Naama Sacagiu-Naor

Fish Can Samba Too

Four Keys for Breakthroughs in Life and Business

Make the right decisions
Discover that anything is possible
Live with passion

Every dream demands someone brave enough who will dare to make it a reality!

First book

© All rights reserved to the author

Phone: 052-5223421

Email: go.to.gdi@gmail.com

Official website: www.totem-d.co.il

Editing: Nurit Harel

Graphic design: Lev Ari Studio

Professional consultation: Amit Offir

Translation: Nava Namdar

No part of the material in this book may be reproduced, copied, photocopied, recorded, translated, stored in a database, transmitted or received in any manner, by any means, electronic, optical or mechanical. Commercial use of any kind of the material contained in this book is strictly prohibited without the express written permission of the author.

Naama Sacagiu-Naor

Fish Can Samba Too

Creating The Reality of Your Dreams

The book was written in the masculine for convenience, but it appeals to both women and men alike.

Table of contents

A moment before we begin 6

How to get the most out of the book 10

Acknowledgements 13

About the author 15

Four Magic Keys 17

Why did I write the book? 21

Forward 24

Part One 26

To dream of Antarctica – To live in the desert
.... 26

   Our lost "hidden dreams" 29

   Dancing with the shadows 36

   Jump on the train towards a new
   opportunity 58

   The 'Dream Realizer Club!' 71

Part Two 76

The quest for the four keys 76

   The secret of the keys 77

The Key of Desire 83

Back to the Great Magician 83

   Awakening to desire 86

   Calibrate the internal compass 95

   The biggest gift shop in the world! 107

The Key of Consciousness 115

When the big picture is revealed 115

Turn insight into a new way of life..... 119

The 'Altitude effect' - making groundbreaking decisions...................... 124

A lesson in reading maps and signs 135

The secret ingredient to a successful consciousness... 144

Key of Transformation.. 156

Map of the Lost Treasure.. 156

How to become Architects of Dreams 161

Put together a successful fulfillment menu.. 173

The recipe for fulfilling dreams........... 181

The Key of Fulfillment.............................. 189

Fish Can Samba Too.. 189

Cast your bread; spread your mission in the world... 193

Look the shadows in the eyes............. 203

This journey is infinite............................. 211

To do the impossible in life and business.. 219

The next step... 222

A moment before we begin

Do you know the feeling of "not quite"? The place where you have a lot, but something is always missing and you have no idea what? The daily routine in which you get up in the morning, go to work, come home in the evening to the place that is supposed to be your sacred sanctuary, and feel a deep inadequacy?

This book is an invitation to all who feel that life is passing them by. In the book, you will find an exciting method I developed over seven years and through which I have reached maximum precision, realization, and fulfillment in my life.

The book combines the key points between my private journey alongside the professional knowledge I acquired that will help you create a real revolution in your life.

In the book, you will find ideas and insights from life experience and awareness, as well as the four keys that will allow you to discover the answer to questions such as: What is missing in my life? How do I bring and ignite passion into my life? How do I turn the Four-Key Model into a way of life that allows me to be the creator of my life?

The book presents you with deep and meaningful ideas that have the power to turn any person into a happier, more successful, and more empowered individual. One who is connected to himself, to his environment, and to his true destiny.

The method presented in the book has become a significant tool that allows me to create countless changes in my life, and today it serves me in my work with business owners.

Through the model, I coach and accompany business owners in the process of developing and building a unique business identity, developing professional and quality products and services, creating a marketing strategy, and developing a brand based on the creation of professional authority. This is all done while maintaining the authenticity and desires of the business owner.

The amazing thing about this method is the ease with which you can achieve results, and the power it has to make your life a more balanced life where the impossible becomes possible.

Proper use of the work model will allow you to input a whole range of considerations into it, to approach every crossroads, and to make any decision from a more exact place and to understand the answer that is most appropriate for you.

Throughout my career as a life coach and business mentor, I have discovered how the method enables the creation of synchronization in all aspects of life, not just for business owners.

Hence the idea of allowing each person to discover his own magic and propel him into his life - whatever it may be - and to bring into it passion, fulfillment, and a significant breakthrough.

This is the first of three books and it brings forward the main points of the method, reveals a new consciousness, and invites you to create real change in all areas of your life.

How to get the most out of the book?

The information in this book is lovingly presented to all who choose to accept it and create a significant change in their lives. **If you are reading these lines, you have chosen to take responsibility for your life and for this, I salute and applaud you.**

In order for you to integrate the ideas and apply the model presented in it, it is important that you do the reading when you are open to absorbing the insights you are about to receive.

The book is divided into five parts that allow you to implement the model in stages. Suggestions and techniques for work are integrated throughout as part of the presentation of the model.

Acquire for yourself the technique of observation. When you have a new idea or are refining an old idea, try to observe it and understand how it is reflected in your personal life: at home, at work, or in business.

Practice the knowledge that is presented to you in this book. Use the personal stories that are integrated into it to gain strength, courage and inspiration, and do not give up even if it challenges you.

Remember: Change is a muscle that is important to strengthen and develop continuously.

Get a notebook and take notes, so you can create your change records and examine your personal growth process throughout reading the book.

Like every change in life and any transformation process, there is a road and a journey to go through.

This book is not an act of magic but contains a life-changing knowledge, so it is recommended that you return to it; to strengthen yourself, to practice, to improve, and to get back on the road, whenever you feel you have lost direction.

And just before you take off, remember: **Nothing is impossible! The only questions are how much do we want it and what are we willing to do to achieve it.**

Acknowledgements

Many acknowledgements and expressions of gratitude need and deserve to be on this page. The greatest of all is **to that brave little girl who resides inside me**. The little girl, who had endured endless challenges, pains, loneliness and sadness, and knew how to use them to grow wings and fly higher and higher.

Thanks to all those people who created challenges and struggles throughout my childhood and adult life, which allowed me to learn who I am, develop the Four-Key Model, and pass it on to the world at large.

Much gratitude to my amazing children, Gefen, Dekel, and Ilan, for always supporting me, reminding me how amazing I am and how proud you are of me, and for being full partners in realizing this dream. I love you eternally!

To my parents, whom each in their own way, serve as a significant milestone in the story of my life. Thanks to them, I became the fulfilled, happy woman I am today.

many thanks to the team at "Best Seller Publishing House" for their professional guidance, support, and great friendship.

And to two very special people sent to me from the heavens: **Lior Atias and Amit Offir**. Thanks to your unceasing support and faith in me, I have been able to build a unique business, fulfill my destiny and myself, and realize the 30-year-old dream of writing this book. **This book is dedicated to all of you with immense love!**

About the author

Naama Sacagiu-Naor is a business consultant specializing in the development and building of breakthrough brands since 2010.

Naama is a life coach, graphic designer, content writer, photographer, and the developer of the Four-Key Method for creating breakthroughs in life. She began her professional career in the field of graphic design and specialized in working with small and medium-sized business owners in the development of the language of their visual brand.

Over the years, Naama has acquired additional expertise and tools that enable her to provide clients with a wide range of professional services and to create for them a complete and holistic package of professional guidance and consultation.

Naama was born in the early 1970's into a challenging reality of a kibbutz in northern Israel. There, she was shaped into a frightened, introverted girl who had lost her way even at the very beginning of her life.

When she became the mother of two small children, her body developed the illness of fibromyalgia, a disease that is manifested in widespread and intense pain as well as many other symptoms. The illness led her to embark on a quest for ways of coping and managing it. Her poignant journey became a quest for personal fulfillment and of a breakthrough that gave birth to a new, strong, fulfilled, and inspirational woman who, on her own merit, created and built a successful and groundbreaking business.

Today, Naama guides and leads individuals and business owners towards a personal and professional breakthrough and helps them create a lifestyle and business management skills based on the principles of passion and fulfillment.

Four Magic Keys

I call them the Four Magic Keys. Four keys that have the power to bring about a tremendous change in the lives of everyone who chooses to use them as a tool for personal fulfillment.

My story begins at the children's home in the kibbutz where I was born.
In the green and serene landscape, I lived a life of constant social alienation, and the assumption with which I entered adulthood was that I had to disappear, be concealed, and be silent.

My only refuge was always the connection to my creativity. Within the world of design, painting, and writing, I found a little respite from the pain and frustration that enveloped me.

As I have grown and matured over the years, most of my childhood memories have been buried away, but inside me, a lost little girl continued to live, dancing with me a dangerous dance, where at times, I managed to lead and flourish and at other times, she took over and returned me back to the starting point.

We danced together in that way for many years, until the day I chose to take the most courageous act of my life, to leave my marriage and embark on a quest to find myself, my identity, and my journey to fulfillment.

From the moment I chose change, I found myself making this choice over and over again because the journeys never conclude but become increasingly more challenging and captivating.

Again and again, I choose anew to delve deep into this special connection between the woman I am today and the lost little girl who is within me and change the rules of the dance.

Many years later, I am now a grown woman. A powerful woman, full of joy for life and with endless optimism, a real warrior, a

single mother with three children, and a business owner of a company that is constantly growing. I can create my own reality and live an authentic life full of action, realization, and fulfillment.

Fish Can Samba Too uniquely combines the story of the lost little girl with the personal and business success story of the woman I am today. **It unlocks a window into my personal growth process**. It brings you the story of the creation of Totem, my private business, which coaches and leads business owners towards breakthroughs in their business. **In this singular book, I present to you a unique method that I have developed over many years, and at its base are the four keys to create change in every field that you choose to bring into your life.**

Each of us has the right to rise at any given moment and to be the person he is meant to be. And if fish can dance the samba, then you too can accomplish everything you dreamed about. The four keys of Totem allow each person to live in fulfillment, contentment, and happiness.

I invite you to go on the journey with me and discover that you too can live a self-realized life, bring authenticity into your daily work and business, and create for yourself a passionate and fulfilled life.

Why did I write the book?

A passion awoke that went deep inside and became a life-changing insight. At the age of 39, something woke up in me, and I started on a special journey of self-discovery. I did not mean for this to happen, but life kept bringing challenging lessons to my door. With these lessons, I embarked on an exciting journey pursuing my passions and dreams and found myself in the center of a powerful personal and business fulfillment.

The more awakened I became, the more I began to feel the universe embracing me. People smiled at me more and sought to be closer to me. One day, I realized that something in my life had reversed. Suddenly, amidst the many internal dialogues I had with the child within me, a new voice had emerged. That voice brought to me the story of an inspiring woman with the ability and courage to withstand great storms and adversity, a woman whose optimism is contagious and who has a great gift to give the world.

I discovered that because of my unique approach to life and having had innumerable challenges, each of which had made me stronger, more capable, and more fulfilled. I realized that my customers' passion is fueled by the business processes I specialize in when they suddenly discover the real powerful purpose that motivates them and the way in which they can turn it into a unique business endeavor. And I understood that there is a way to extract the substance from which I am built and bring with its help a great gift to a great many people.

The dream of writing a book has been waiting for the right moment since I was a 14-year-old girl. I remember dreaming of the day when I would write the story of my life and the great excitement that took hold of me each time anew. Somehow, over the years, the hope of writing was forgotten in my drawer of hidden dreams and waited quietly for the right moment.

Why now? Because today I have a precise method, experience using this method, professional knowledge, and the courage to pass it on. There is no better time than now to give this to you as a gift so that you too can embark on a journey of fulfillment.

Forward

The last moving box was sealed with transparent tape. I looked at the high stack of cardboard boxes that cluttered the small living room in my home, inside of which were packed 40 years of my life. Tears flooded my eyes, an uncontrollable sobbing shook my body, and an ocean of questions rose and floated inside me.

Here I closed the door on a 12-year-old relationship and started the transition into the unknown. I knew that at the end of the road a new door would be waiting for me, but when would I get to that door? What was waiting for me behind the door? What if I have not tried enough? What if my decision was a mistake? And what would happen to my business? What can be waiting for someone who leaves a complete life, continues with a failed business, works for pennies and has been lost in the journey of life?

With tears in my eyes, I got up and began dragging boxes into the small children's room. I gathered my strength, moved the furniture inside, and closed the door behind me. Forty years of wandering had ended and something new was about to begin in a week. I picked up the large garbage bags containing dozens of objects that had been with me throughout my life, turned off the light, and went out into the cool night.

Tomorrow, the renovation would begin. New energy would enter my house and my journey towards my new life would begin.

A big smile formed on my face. Something inside me had begun to wake up…

Part One

To dream of Antarctica – To live in the desert

"A person can spend a whole lifetime searching, while the truth lies deep within him, waiting for that one moment of courage to break out and emerge".

The quiet sound of the waves woke me slowly from my sleep. I turned over in bed and a little smile came over my lips. My Nikon camera grinned at me from atop the dresser, waiting for me to take it in my hand and go on a wild adventure on this enchanting little beach I had reached on my journey to southern Italy.

I stretched my body slowly like a tiger waking up from an afternoon siesta and stepped out of my room to the balcony overlooking the small, pristine beach. I needed nothing more than this blessed silence, the melody of the sea, the magnificent view, and a camera hanging around my neck.

What else does a man need than to follow his heart and connect to his true passions, and those that breathe life into him and allow him to live a fuller, more fulfilling and satisfying life?

With a clear, ancient knowledge, my thoughts began to arrange themselves into place with no words. The inner place hidden inside me became calm as the countless sounds and noises settled down, and the sea continued to sing a love song to me.

I closed my eyes in the hypnotic landscape, turned my hand into a fist, and summoned the key to me. The key to the treasure chest, filled with all my hidden dreams, that I had locked up many years ago. The dreams I was afraid to dream aloud, the ones that embarrassed me, and those I thought were a few sizes too big for me and stopped believing could ever come true.

My surroundings and the social conventions in my place of residence made me believe for many years that my powers were limited and that my starting positions in life were very low compared with the chest filled with passions and hidden dreams.

I could feel something new flowing in my veins and spreading through my body. Suddenly it stood there, my golden treasure chest. Slowly I reached for it and lifted the heavy lid. My hidden dreams began to soar, painting the air with vibrant colors as they twirled around me, caressing me with their gentle wings, as if to say, "Take us with you on the journey of your life".

Our lost "hidden dreams"

Within each of us, lives a little being who buries and hides our dreams away and whose job is to bring our lives into line and adapt them to what is right and "correct" according to the social standards in which we live. This Concealer of Dreams holds the key to the box and keeps it away so that dreams do not escape from it, lest they turn our lives upside down.

Let us talk for a moment about our dreams, the reason why there are so many unrealized dreams in our world, and about the people who live a whole lifetime with a sense of loss and missing out.

Sometimes we dream of natural and small things like finding a loving relationship and having a family, learning how to play a musical instrument or paint, or travelling around the world. But quite a few of us envision the really big dreams, like changing the world, designing a new invention on a global scale, doing work that we really love, and creating a business built entirely of what we love to do.

Our dreams are a collection of what we love, our abilities, and our desires which yearn to come out and help us live a fuller, happier, and more complete life. Their role is to connect us to our inner world, and to enable us to find the things that will make us happy and have a realized life of real enthusiasm and passion.

When I think about how there are so many dreams and opportunities waiting for a moment of realization in our world, I have quite a few basic questions, which allow me to create a different reality for myself, a reality in which I live my passions continuously.

I examine these questions every day anew, whether it is in my personal life or while leading business owners in the creation of a unique, successful, and groundbreaking business that they can operate out of passion and a sense of mission.

In this chapter, I will talk about the Concealer of Dreams and answer questions such as:

- What prevents us from setting out to fulfill our dreams?
- What is the reason that thousands of people give up on self-realization and fulfillment?
- What causes business owners with vision and potential to despair along the way and shut down their business?

During my challenging childhood years in the kibbutz, I developed a mechanism for pleasing the people around me. I put myself aside constantly and was and did whatever others wanted me to be and do. It will be more accurate to say, "tried to be", because the truth is, I never succeeded at it. No matter how much I tried, I was always an outsider within the group of children I grew up with. I was the target of humiliation, ridicule, and physical and verbal violence. It was so arduous that I began to disappear into myself. When they laughed at my voice, I stopped talking. When they laughed at the way I looked, I began to wear oversized clothing, trying to hide myself. And when I was told that I would never find a loving partner because I was nothing, I stopped believing in love. In fact, in my first 18 years of life, I chose to put all my dreams and desires into a box and bury it deep, just so I could save myself from myself.

When I wanted to talk to someone, I would talk quietly to myself as I walked along the pathways of the kibbutz, telling myself stories about different a time to come; the time when I would open the chest and these dreams would come out one by one. On the kibbutz, I would stop from time to time and make sure I was still alone on the path before continuing to speak aloud to myself to dull the frustrating sense of loneliness.

Many years have passed. Only at the age of 39, when I was already a wife and a mother of three children, did I dare to look back and understand what had happened, and slowly open the chest that had been waiting for me for years, buried deep in the sand.

The alarming fact that millions of people all over the world spend their whole lives without experiencing real happiness and tens of thousands of business owners close their businesses every year raises questions.

What motivates a person to get up in the morning and launch into a challenging business activity? Is good income enough

to create happiness and personal satisfaction? Is a college degree or profession a guarantee of success? And what is success? What are the criteria for measuring it?

Throughout my years of working with and leading business owners to breakthroughs in their businesses, I discovered that our world is divided into two types of people:

- **Those who choose their way out of necessity and reality**, surrender to social conventions, live their lives exactly according to the expectations of the environment, and create for themselves a conventional life on a predictable path but lack fulfillment and self-realization.

    Sooner or later, these people feel inexplicable emptiness. It seems like there is always something missing in their lives, and they find it difficult to pinpoint where this feeling of discomfort comes from.

If you belong in this group, you will receive cognitive and practical tools from this book that will help you change your way of life and bring you fulfillment and satisfaction.

- **Those who choose their way while connecting to their passion** are the people who are connected to their work and act out of true passion. They make choices in their lives by connecting to their truth, even when it seems strange to their immediate or distant surroundings. They know how to combine their skills and their loves with the choice of a new job or while creating a business. They understand the importance of living purposeful lives and they create meaning for themselves in life.

If you are among these people, you already know that it is not always easy to go "your own way" and that sometimes you may find yourself swimming against the current and hearing your dream suppressor trying to hinder you on the way. But, you also know that there is nothing more empowering than the moment you achieve your goal in your own way.

In this book, you will find four keys that will help you build greater pathways of growth and fulfillment, develop precision throughout the process, and find a way to make the journey easier for you.

Now that you have identified where you stand and what group of people you belong to, let us talk about the Hider of Dreams and those factors that delay us on the way to fulfillment.

Dancing with the shadows

If we lived in a Utopian world, we would experience events of perpetual fulfillment and satisfaction. We would have more precision, be able to create a life of fulfillment for ourselves, personal expression and realization, and would continue to grow and develop in all areas of life: work, family life, personal and business development and more.

The search for that ideal world occupies the lives of quite a lot of people around the world. Most live a life dictated to them by social conventions. The majority conceal their dreams in a deep box and carefully hide the key to avoid it ever being discovered, and alongside the routine life they live, there is a constant internal struggle between those hidden desires and dreams and the facts dictated to them by reality.

That is exactly how millions of people find themselves, in someone else's life. These people are turning around a central axis of self-searching, trying to find that inner precision and start living a fuller and more satisfying life.

One of the greatest tasks in my personal and professional life was to find the answer to the question: How could I realize myself at any given moment? After so many years in which I did not know who I was, there was great desire in me to fill-in the big gaps. To live, to experience, to taste, to try, to face my fears, and to conquer more and more mountain peaks. Life is too short to stand still.

Ever since I discovered the woman who has been hidden inside me for so many years, I have had a strong need to turn my life's journey into a method of changing life and to give it as a gift to the world, with the knowledge that this will allow millions of people to wake up, discover the beauty within them, and begin to offer and spread their own gifts in the world.

The people around me said that I was like a bulldozer, and it was hard to keep up with me. Some of them said that I lacked focus, some warned me to not expose myself too much because I was liable to get hurt, that I should not take financial risks because I could fail financially, that I should not hurt my children on the way, and that I should not fall apart. Some of them (those who belong to my past world) stood confused, sometimes disdainful, or renounced the changes that have taken place in me.

There were so many voices facing one pure truth that could no longer be held captive inside. From the moment that truth became consciousness, my life changed beyond recognition.

Time and again, strong winds arrived, and I found myself swinging between a convenient possibility to give up on everything and go back to hiding in my familiar shell, or to have the courage to fight the demons and continue on the path even when it is frightening, sad, difficult, and lonely.

If I gave up, what was the purpose of all the years of suffering and loneliness that shaped the woman I am today? And if I chose to fight, I could give the little girl inside me a life lesson and could heal her wounded soul just a little bit more. I would live fully. I would really live my life just as I chose to live it and be whole!

Just like me, most people are aware of their process of shelving away their dreams. They feel that something within them is missing and are paralyzed in the face of the idea that something in their routine will change. That a new door would open and behind it, the unknown.

So why do most of us live so far away from a sense of fulfillment and personal satisfaction, and how can we create a method that will allow everyone to live a life full of passion and fulfillment at any given moment?

When we face a situation of uncertainty, the oldest defense mechanism begins to operate:

The building of high walls of excuses and reasons why not; why it will not work, why it is not the time, why it is not financially possible, and more.

As uncertainty grows and fear begins to run through us, our list of excuses expands and grows until it becomes a whole defense system that dissolves the little chance within us, the courage to open the chest of dreams and begin to change.

And then, this happens: just like magic, we begin to hear the voices from the shadows and the sounds that show us how right we are to have defenses to protect ourselves. That we do not have a chance, that the economic situation is too difficult, and that our protective wall is keeping us safe from all the terrible things that can happen. And we find ourselves imprisoned behind that wall day after day, looking out through a tiny crack into an entire world of beauty and fulfillment, dreaming of the moment when we will have the courage to break out and go free.

She came to the informational meeting, sat down and asked me:
"So what do you do?"
"Wait", I said "tell me a little about yourself, your business, your dream, where do you want to go?"

She shared with me. I asked deliberate questions and wrote down important points so that I could give her the service that would advance her in the most precise and beneficial way.

She spoke in such a low voice, as if she did not believe in herself and that it could really happen. I could feel as if something inside her was shrinking as she continued to speak.

"So what do you do?" She asked me when she finished telling me about her clinic, the difficult challenges she faced, and the hopes and dreams she had.

I patiently explained to her what I did and where I could take her and her business and her eyes lit up with excitement. Not because of me, but because I envisioned for her the tremendous leap she could make in her business.

I talked about the importance of a digital marketing system for therapists and my work method with the four keys. I talked about opening the barrier that stopped customers from reaching her and the way in which she could change from being an absolute stranger in the network, to a well-known, recognized, and valued professional authority. I talked about the opportunity to create digital information products that would establish the business's reputation and provide significant additional income.

She sat across from me and listened. I could feel her building a high defensive wall around her, pushing my words back and away as if afraid to let them absorb into her consciousness.

When I was done, she said, embarrassed,
"I thought you might do things differently."
I smiled and explained that I was indeed doing things differently. The method I had created,

what guides me in my work, and the tools I have are all different."

She continued, not allowing the words to penetrate, "I do not connect to all this digital stuff". I explained to her gently that there was no magic, this was a prelude, and she could choose to stay behind or boldly open the door to the new world.

She thanked me in a weak voice, and I felt how the enormity of the possible change paralyzed her completely.

"But how do we start?" she suddenly asked.
"Start by choosing yourself", I said, looking into her eyes. "The moment you choose you, I will be there by your side," I smiled.

This woman was about to give up. She almost let go of the opportunity to face and grow into a new place. However, I was able to dissolve her fears and help her embark on an exciting journey of development and growth. Today, she is no longer afraid of the digital world but knows how to leverage it for her business and enjoy the many possibilities it provides. This process saved her clinic from closing down, significantly increased the number of patients, and created passive income from the information products she sells online.

This meeting echoed in my mind for a long time. I suddenly realized how sensitive the process of developing a business could be. How many shadows and fears can overwhelm a business owner standing alone facing a world of marketing so wide and demanding.

I realized how our modern world, which is well understood to me, could be threatening to someone else. I also realized how important it was for me to be there to accompany, guide, build the right foundations, and gradually dispel the fears until they became a distant history.

That day, I received two gifts. First: the opportunity to guide my client and her business to growth. Second: a very important life-lesson that not all of us are made of the same material, but we all have the ability to choose to create another reality for ourselves.

The message I got from that meeting echoed in me for a few weeks afterwards.
I realized that people who want to get different results from what they receive over and over again, those who dream of breaking the glass ceiling in their lives, whether it is in their business or in any other field, must put into their work a new component and change the equation so that their results will change.

I also understood how important it was to elevate the courage needed to achieve fulfillment with complete openness and the willingness to dance with our shadows in order for us to learn how to turn those that would hold us back into a tool to bring down the high wall of defense and make our story a success story.

So what really stops us from getting what we want for ourselves? What are the shadows that are obstacles to the lives of our dreams, the parts of us that if we know how to dance with in the right way, we can then release the barriers that stop us?

The ways in which our dreams go into hiding are through a variety of voices, limiting beliefs, fears, and lack of support from our immediate surroundings. All of these build our defense walls that, over the years, become an inseparable part of us. The walls create a thick, impenetrable armor that harms all aspects of our lives.

When we are enveloped in this thick armor, our chances of succeeding in life are nil. We become people who are drifting with the current and do not have the ability to navigate the ship of our lives to the port we dream of arriving at.

How can you be set free of this heavy armor?

The first stage is the mapping stage. There are two types of shadows. the shadows that come to us from the outside and those from within.

Let us get to know some of the shadows that accompany us, and the effect they have on our lives:

Our internal range of shadows: These include our fears, limiting beliefs about ourselves, and all the stories we tell ourselves.

- **Fear of failure:** Most people see the experience of failure as a humiliating, crushing, and very difficult experience. The fear is of the experience of pain. What will people say about me? What I will say about myself?

- **Fear of success:** The desired success brings with it quite a few struggles and compromises in life. It requires us leaving our comfort zone, investment in time and money, sacrifices, and more. Many people interpret success as arrogance, conceit, and stepping on others backs. Uncertainty over questions such as, Who am I going to turn into should I become a successful person? Will I be able to remain the person I am today? What price will I have to pay? All these create great fear. If untreated, it changes from a welcomed defense mechanism into a mechanism of destroying dreams.

- **Lack of Motivation** - Motivation is the power that drives a person to strive towards achieving his goals. The fuel that drives motivation is desire and passion. When we know exactly what our desires are and can feel them stirring up inside us, motivation ignites within us. When we discover what our desire is, new shadows are often born and try to extinguish it.

Once a conflict has been created between our now conscious desires and the reality of our lives that does not match these desires, a process begins of a loss of energy and lack of motivation in all areas of life. It is similar to a car with an empty tank that keeps moving on just fuel fumes.

- **Lack of earnestness and commitment:** Many people dream of being, doing, and conquering mountaintops. **Few are willing to devote themselves to the process and its fruition.** We are very good at telling ourselves stories. We are great at living in an imaginary world where everything comes to us easily. But are we ready to commit ourselves and follow our dreams to completion, even if it means continuing against all odds?

Lack of seriousness and a lack of commitment are two sides of the same coin. The excuses are so many that it is difficult to count them; financial obstacles, not enough time, not the right time, illnesses, and more. So in the absence of serious commitment and the willingness to persist and follow through, the right time to get up and take a courageous step never arrives.

- **Limiting beliefs:** Each of us has a small child within that always reminds us of everything we have been told and taught. When a child hears a parental authority figure say things such as "You are so silly." or "You are never going to succeed". or "You look like a little monkey", he internalizes these statements into himself. A child cannot make the distinction between joking and seriousness, between right and wrong, and something inside him gets deeply wounded.

As a result, his subconscious is embedded with undermining thoughts and limiting beliefs that ground him and render him immobile.

Each of us goes into adulthood with these faulty thoughts, and these beliefs come out at a precise time to keep us away from our passion and purpose.

- **Self-manipulation:** The art of self-convincing is one of the strongest shadows. This art is the way of which we convince ourselves that all the feelings we feel, our unfulfilled desires that bubble up to the surface and create emptiness within us, are just our imagination. We tell ourselves that our lives are full and wonderful and that we need to be grateful for what we have instead of look for something new and exciting. These stories have the power to distract and divert us from the path of fulfillment.

- **Lack of determination and perseverance:** To live a life of fulfillment is to embark on an exciting journey, and as in any journey, perseverance is the name of the game. Whether our dream is personal or about business, we have a journey ahead and the length of time it will take is not always known.

The road to fulfillment is a little like playing chutes and ladders, there are quite a few surprises waiting for us. At times, we leap forward and at other times, we take a few steps back. In order to get through the game, we need to have the right determination that will enable us to be unwavering, to persevere, and to continue on the road again and again.

Our external range of shadows: The debilitating influence of external factors and our environment on our daily decision-making and managing.

- **Lack of learning and knowledge:** Lack of knowledge equals lack of confidence on our journey. It brings failures and depleting experiences that immediately trigger personal mechanisms of defense that weaken us, extinguish our passion and determination, and cause us to shelve our dreams, sometimes forever.

- **Education and social environment**: The education we received from an early age, the place we live in, and the society to which we belong; all these create a whole set of behavioral patterns and social norms. These are some of the most important elements in how most people operate. **The great majority goes with the norm even if the heart tells them otherwise.**

The fear of: What will be said about me? How will society respond to me? Will I still belong if I choose to live in a different way than everyone else around me? How will this affect my family and my social life? When we live by the standards of the society around us, we are forced to make countless small and big compromises within ourselves.

- **External Manipulations:** Manipulations are a tricky matter. They are very difficult to distinguish, but they have a very strong influence on our decision-making. Since they are often "invisible", they can come under the guise of one small word, which triggers a particularly destructive mechanism within us and causes us to make a decision that does not benefit us.

How many times have you purchased something you did not really want? The gut said one thing and the head chose another. At how many crossroads in your life did you turn in the opposite direction from what your instincts said because your mom exerted pressure, your partner seemed unhappy, the community began murmuring? External manipulations are one of the heaviest shadows that hold us back from growth and fulfillment.

A person who follows the mandates of the shadows within and around him, prevents himself from being able to see the many opportunities that surround him and to identify which ones can bring him to a place of fulfillment. If he can see the opportunities, he finds himself frozen in front of them without the ability to leverage them into a life-changing action.

The price paid by those who choose not to face their shadows is very high!

I was then a mother of two small babies, living with my partner in the kibbutz I chose to return to despite the difficult childhood in which I grew up. I was surrounded by greenery, by peace and calm. That is what I told myself back then. On the surface, I had no reason to tell myself another story. But the shadows inside and around me worked overtime, gnawing away at my real ambitions, my destiny, and all that excites and inspires me, dissolving it all into an imaginary world that even I did not dare open.

I worked at the kibbutz supermarket as deputy director. I managed orders and suppliers, sent invoices, and was great at customer service. I earned a paltry salary, but I was happy (at least in appearance).

Today, I can say that at that time I was like a walking dead with my eyes closed. My patience with people was non-existent, and the nervousness and impatience were always attributed to my red headed temper. But the truth was different. Deep inside me, something was missing. Something was bubbling in me and was looking for a way out of the locked box. Slowly and quietly, my frustration grew bigger, without my knowing it, nor giving it words. Then, one day something happened.

My body started to speak. It began with a strange shortness of breath that grew worse every day.

There were days when I would sit down on the floor in the middle of the store dizzy, gasping for air, trying to regulate my breathing. It did not take long for me to begin experiencing severe pains. The pain was not focused and was burning and torturing me 24/7.

I knew something was very wrong with my body, but I did not understand what my body was trying to say. With two babies at home and an inability to function, I began to think of serious illnesses and fearful stories overwhelmed me. Months of physical tests have not yielded any conclusions as to the reason for the pain. Medically, I was healthy, but my body was screaming with all its might.

Five long, agonizing years passed before I received a diagnosis. I had fibromyalgia. After learning to pronounce the strange name that became a part of me, I found myself delighted! I felt happy that I finally knew what I was dealing with (I thought I knew), certain that conventional medicine would cure me, and I could go back to my daily routine.

But the reality was different. The more I took painkillers and the more I tried alternative medicine, the more I found myself falling apart. Doing research on the disease, I discovered a worrisome statistic. There is no solution, although there is a possibility of alleviating it, and I had exhausted all the solutions to alleviate the pain. I found myself helpless in the face of reality. Months have gone by, and my functioning was deteriorating. But the weaker my body became, the stronger and more resolute my mind was to fight this disease to its end. It was only a matter of time before something good would happen after I made that decision. The change came as a complete surprise.

You could say I redheaded even notice that it happened.
One evening, while at a meeting of business owners trying to test the viability of starting my own business, I ran into a very special person.

Everyone around was whispering that he could cure people from illnesses, so I decided to try.

Standing boldly and daring to look directly into your own eyes and soul is a defining moment, and that is exactly what happened to me. The man informed me from the outset that everything I had been told about him was not true, and he had no idea how to cure people. He did, however, know how to help people look deep inside and find the answers they are looking for. The series of meetings with him after this initial conversation brought an upheaval into my life.

I began to look within, seeing everything that was sad, frightening, and obstructive. I suddenly discovered that I was living someone else's life. For years, I have been pleasing my surroundings just to minimize the chance of getting hurt. Ihad been hurt so many times in my life, and I discovered that I simply gave up on myself and my right to be what I really wanted to be.

My spirit was enveloped in thick layers of self-criticism and external disapproval, in a heavy layer of fear, appeasement, and prejudice from the inside and the outside. Somewhere deep inside, I hid, cut off from the world. I was unaware of the destructive process that was going on in my soul, which was burdened by this heavy load for years until it began to scream and shout to the body to warn it that she was breaking, shattering to small pieces.

There is something reassuring about standing with your eyes open to reality, as difficult and challenging as it may be. Once you understand the reality of your life, you can choose change and create a new, happier, more successful, and satisfying life, a life of fulfillment.

In order to create a real change in your life, you have to go through two primary processes after which you can embark on a journey of self-discovery:

First, you must reach an understanding that you are in a place that is not right for you, and the **second**, is to make a real and courageous decision to change the reality of your life and create for yourself a different existence.

Jump on the train towards a new opportunity

There are those who jump on a train bravely and travel to new places, and there are those who think and deliberate until the train disappears on the horizon and they remain on the platform, disappointed and frustrated.

A great deal of courage is required of a person to face his naked soul and observe. This is exactly where all manner of shadows rise up and submerge us, threatening to consume us if we dare to stand up and say, "It is my turn now."

More than once in my life, I felt as if I was lying down on the railroad tracks, feeling the wheels cut through my soul as the train passed over me and continued on its way. Many years passed before I dared to get up, take responsibility for my life, bandage my wounds, and choose change.

The change in my life was a process. I learned to identify the points where the disease worsened. I learned to see what was going on inside of me. What part of my soul was trampled and disregarded. I taught myself to stand boldly in my truth and voice it loudly and fully, make the right choices for me, and build myself up.

It was a journey of falling in love! Suddenly my life was painted in new vibrant colors. Shades I did not know existed in me. And so, I found myself in the middle of studying to be a graphic designer and decided to devote myself to this passion. I informed my husband that I was leaving my job at the supermarket and opening a design studio. It was against all logic. At first, the studio did not make any money, but it was more authentic than anything else I had chosen to do in my life.

So, on an old impulse that could not remain suppressed any longer, I made the decision that I later understood had changed the whole course of my life. As the days passed, I gradually began to realize that all the pains of the disease, which had accompanied me for many years, had disappeared as if they never were and instead were replaced with creativity and feelings of freedom and fulfillment. The challenges that I had to operate and elevate the business filled every corner of my soul and it became liberated.

The insight that has resonated in me since that day and directs my path in life and my professional road is that **a person who acts out of his passions, lives an authentic life, and chooses the course of his life out of the truth**

within him, is a happy and successful person. Yes, the universe opens doors and supports those who have the courage to choose themselves despite all the challenges on the way.

This insight changed my life beyond recognition! It was my first step in a long and challenging road that allowed me to go out into the world in all my radiant colors.

Most of the world's population is living in a cycle of unrealized life: emptiness, fear of doing anything, ignoring their internal voices, and so on.

Many people shy away from the change that happens when they dare to go within and observe, but this is precisely where the road to change begins.

The consequences of not dealing with issues that discourage us are harsh. It turns us into hand-held puppets and pulls away our belief in ourselves, our passions, and joy. What comes into our lives instead is a darkness that prevents us from creating a path for ourselves and expressing what we have come to give to the world.

And when people live on the peripheries of life, real chaos is created in the world. Darkness penetrates us, and we begin to get lost within ourselves and within existence.

This fear of change is one of the greatest dream suppressors of our lives!

People can live a whole lifetime without knowing who they are and what they can do. They can get up every morning; do the same things over and over again in a disappointing routine, and dream about another life without daring to put their feet on the path that will lead them to happiness.

Unhappy people are people who are angrier, hopeless, prone to furious outbursts, without a zest for life, and are disposed to extreme and objectionable actions. It is no wonder that we live in a crazy world. We are witnessing wars, corruption, abuse, and severe violence in our world and are forced to pay harsh personal and social costs.

It sounds discouraging and impossible, but the truth is that there is a way. There is a hidden set of keys within each person that will enable you to open the door and embark on a journey of change.

How to find the set of keys? If you feel frustrated, disappointed, and discouraged. If you feel that something is not right in your life, that you want something else but do not dare to make a change, or maybe you do not even know what it is that will change your life and make it a life of fulfillment and satisfaction - Congratulations! You have just won the title of 'The Perpetual Dreamer'!

This title gives you the right to enter a new and exciting arena. This arena is where people learn to find the set of keys hidden deep inside and access their dream chest.

In order to enter the arena, the only two things that you are required to do are: agreeing to look within yourself even if it is difficult and choosing to make a real change in your life.

Know that choosing to change does not mean that you have to do extreme things like getting a divorce or leaving your job. Real change means that going forward, you will learn to make your choices from a place of authenticity and passion, which you will discover throughout the journey.

Along the journey, you will be able to avail yourself of quite a few lifelines. Lifelines that will illuminate your way when you are facing a dilemma, help you make the right decisions, and will protect you from the dream hiders, who will often try to bring you back to the beginning.

Like the dream hiders, your lifelines are divided in two. Those who are within you (even if you are unaware of them) and those who can assist you from the outside and whose main task is to show you your inner strength and that you are your own savior.

Who are those external supporting forces that can assist?

- **Close friends or family members:** Be sure to choose those who believe in you and are able to support and advise without judgment. The line between a friend who will help you advance and a friend who will bring you down is very thin.

- **Acquiring knowledge and skills:** Do you remember? Knowledge equals strength and power equals precision filled choices. When you are at a crossroads, you feel frightened, confused, or that you lack enough information enough information. It is time to sign on to Google and get the information you need. Register for a professional or informational course that will broaden your horizons, or buy a book that can provide you with the knowledge needed and give you the confidence to continue on the way.

- **Find inspirational sources:** Follow people who have already made it. These people are all around us and can serve as a source of strength for you and provide you with life-changing insights.

- **Hire a professional life coach:** Travelling in two is always easier. Do not be afraid to ask for help from a professional who specializes in personal development and can accompany you throughout the journey.

These professionals can lift you up if you fall, strengthen you if you break down, and more importantly, help you find the inner supports that exist within you and teach you how to correctly use them and create a new reality for yourself.

- **The people of the 'Why yes'**: These special people will always find the most creative solutions even when it seems that none exist. To break through and create change, it is important that you surround yourself with the right energies. Fill your world with people who have already done what you want to do. Those who will always find the right word and the way to lift you up. Those who know what is required for a man to go through his journey.

Once you have made the choice, a window of opportunity is created that allows you to break through the merry-go-round in which most people are trapped and create for yourself exactly the way of life you dream about. All you have to do is make sure the road is clear. When there is clarity in your life, something new begins to happen.

Suddenly you discover inner lifelines and powers you were not aware of. These will come in the form of your skills, the things you love to do, your strengths, and your ability to think outside the box and find creative ways that will bring you the solutions and opportunities that will help you create exactly the right change you are seeking.

It is important to understand that there are no shortcuts on the journey. In order for the insights and methods you will learn throughout the journey to become a real and permanent way of life, it is very important to have perseverance, determination and patience, and train yourself to constantly face the new consciousness that is about to enter your life.

Once you have understood where you want to go, designate your big goal. Ask yourself what is the final destination you are aiming towards. From there, you will obtain the intermediate goals that will allow you to ascend towards the goal that is now at the top of the mountain.

This is true in your life and this is true in your business.

Your fulfillment is guaranteed – Starting the moment you adjust your understanding that everything begins and ends with your thinking patterns and your ability to train yourself and build a strong, empowering mechanism based on your inner world.

Beginning the moment you set clear goals and objectives for yourself aimed at bringing you to the summit step by step.

Once you have created a work plan, pack a backpack with boldness, determination, courage, perseverance and belief in yourself. Choose to go on the road and take at least one step towards your goals each day.

It went on for years. I was married and a mother of two children, right at the beginning of my journey, beginning to discover my abilities and dreams, and running a small business that was just born. And he? Well, he was who he was. We met in a business-networking group and quickly became good friends. We had years of close friendship, the kind you cannot find every day. Wholesome, pure friendship I call it, but there was always something that was not communicated.

One New Year's Eve, there was a strange twist in the friendship between us, from one Facebook message to another. He was already divorced and in a new relationship, and I was a mother of three and separated from my partner. Suddenly, there was an understanding that both of us felt what had never been spoken.

I, who had already come a long way in my private journey, found myself entangled in an impossible relationship. There was no doubt in our long and intimate conversations what he wanted. But along with the desire came great fear, and the defensive wall went up.

It went on in this way for several years. We separated and came together again knowing that only the making of a real decision could end the exhausting ritual in which we were involved in: passions and yearnings, dreams and fears, heartache, disappointment and great frustration.

The gap between us grew. The wholesome, stress-free friendship split in two. He sat on the platform, watching trains pass by and daydreamed, and I was ready to jump on the train with him and embark on a journey of joint discovery.

I kept waiting for him, giving him countless opportunities. Finally, I gave up and got on the train alone to discover new worlds. I discovered myself in countless moments and struggles.

And he was left behind, disappointed and carrying within himself a sense of missed opportunity and the knowledge that he was not brave enough.

From time to time, the train stops again at the same station, and he is still sitting there on the bench dreaming. For a quick moment that turns shorter each time, I open a small window again, reach out to him from the train, and invite him to jump in with me. To give up the fear and be moved by the power of discovery, but I remain alone. Willing to pay the price of his choices and continue on my way.

In my travels, I learned that there are roads that will never meet, yet some will eventually intersect and become a common way. I have also learned how important it is to take the first step courageously, against all odds, and how wondrous worlds arrive on the paths of our lives if only we dare.

Once you discover your inner strengths and learn to use them to create a real change in life, and to live a life of passion and fulfillment, you will be promoted and can join the 'Dream Realizer Club'.

The 'Dream Realizer Club!'

Fulfillment is not just the moment when you stand on the summit but an endless process of growth, development, and expansion. Realization is the constant climb over mountain peaks. At times, you will have to go down in order for you to conquer the next peak. At other times, you will have to deal with a fierce shadow attack. But once you have chosen to be in the Dream Realizer Club, there will be nothing to stop you from marching forward!

The only admittance ticket to the Dream Realizer Club is you choosing to become a member. The moment when you decide to dedicate yourself and walk with your truth to the end and persevere against all odds, to stand firm against every challenge and obstacle, to cross a stormy river, to climb mountains, and to not stop even once, is the moment you will enter into a new, empowering, and exciting world of creation.

In a moment, I will reveal to you the Four-Key Method for the first time. I developed this method over seven years, and it serves as a tool to coach and lead business owners and individuals in the processes of change and creation of higher quality and a more authentic life.

Proper use of this method and its integration as a way of life will enable you to do the impossible and create the reality you dream of.

The method was born and developed from my own journey, which I embarked on when I was sick, desperate, and frustrated in every area I looked at. This is by far the most stunning and progressive discovery of my life.

Turning it into a daily way of life brought me to new levels of internal and physical balance, awakened in me new strengths that I was not aware of, and turned me into a professional pathfinder.

What do I mean by defining myself as a professional pathfinder? The ability to get up every morning anew and choose the path that is right for me to walk on today, next month, and in the coming year. The ability to create a precise map that will lead me safely to each destination, knowing that at each junction on the road, I will be able to calibrate myself, connect to this fascinating method, and choose the right direction for me.

But let us go back to the beginning for a moment.

From the moment that the insight began to reverberate in me that a person who acts out of his passions was living a more authentic and healthy life, I realized that my illness was the greatest gift I had ever received in my life. It arrived to awaken me from a long sleep and deep internal freeze. Something inside me began to thaw.

It was a sharp and quick change. Once I understood that it was time to open my dream chest up and that this was the only remedy that would allow me to get better, a new woman was born within me. She was determined, optimistic, and motivated to find the key to that box, the chest of my hidden dreams.

Many insights accompanied my search and every insight brought with it another gift. In those days, I was the mother of a small trio of children and had a small business at its outset. I opened my studio from an unconscious place, and in an impulsive way, followed a weak inner voice that grew stronger over the years.

That inner knowledge that connected me to a new source of energy and enabled me to see the right path was so empowering and powerful that all I had left to do was boldly face my habits, choose to act differently, and free myself from everything that bound and kept me aground.
 The choices in my life became increasingly strange to the outside observer but more authentic to me, and the more I dared to look deeper, the more the road became clearer.

The Four-Key Method brings with it a great message to all those who have chosen to enter the Dream Realizer Club. Its function is to create a balance between the four layers that make up the complete fulfillment process.

What is the Four-Key Method? How can it be transformed into a way of life that will enable you to live in continuous fulfillment?

How can you realize your personal, professional, and family dreams using it?

What is the true power of this life-changing tool?

Let us dive into the secret of the four keys and discover their magic.

Part Two

The quest for the four keys

"And when you reach the finish line and you have the magic keys in your hands, a wide horizon opens up to you and you stand facing a land of endless opportunities."

The secret of the keys

In this section, I will present to you the Four-Key Method and the unique worldview behind it.

Each key has an important role to play in the process of using the method, and creating a proper synchronization between the four keys will enable the achievement of significant results in every field of life in which you choose to implement the method. It is therefore important to understand in depth the role of each key within the larger framework.

Let us get to know the four keys so we can understand the worldview behind each of them and the right work method that will enable you to activate your own personal breakthrough mechanism:

1. **The Key of Desire:** This is the first key in the method where you will find the

deep answers, and the power that will drive you towards fulfillment. Here you will find the connection between your mission and the innate "work tools" given to you, so you can realize yourself in the most authentic way.

Your desires, values, talents, strengths, and abilities all provide you with great power that, when used correctly, can help you understand your mission and plan for its fulfillment.

Once you understand what your mission is and the innate tools you have in order to realize it, a new space is created that enables you to take your unique elements and create a special self-realization process.

2. **The Key of Consciousness:** This is the key that connects your innate tools to the world of reality. It enables them to turn into raw materials that can be conveyed in words, turns them into a

personal process or a crystallized business idea, and begins to process them into a new and cohesive awareness that can be applied in practice.

One of the best ways to turn a collection of desires into an idea with applied potential is to understand the meaning behind them and make them a way of life and an integral part of your awareness.

3. **The Key of Transformation:** This key is responsible for the planning and strategy development process through which you can realize your ideas and mission. Here is where to put your innate tools into the planning process and discover how to turn them into significant tools that will allow you to create a unique and precise way and put together your own path of fulfillment.

At the completion of the planning stage, the "realization plan" of the project you chose will be revealed to you. A new and precise direction will then allow you to start on the new path you have unlocked for yourself.

4. **The Key of Fulfillment:** Once you have the first three keys that form your realization plan, it is now time to become a project manager and bring your passion-filled work plans into action.

This project management is the fourth key, and its job is to turn your plans into reality. This is the exciting stage in which you actualize your personal or business dream and increase the light and positive energies within you. The more you become empowered and grow, the greater the light and energies of those around you grow. From there, wide ripples spread throughout the world.

Practicing and implementing the method on a regular basis will enable you to create countless groundbreaking paths and have the ability to achieve more and more in your personal and professional life, whether you are an independent business owner or a salaried employee, and have the ability to achieve more and more in your personal and business goals. If you choose to use the four keys and make them a way of life, you will be surprised to discover that you have become "unstoppable", driven by tremendous power and an everlasting fire.

How have I made this model an integral part of my life, and how can you do it in your life?

You are invited to dive with me to the enchanted world of the four keys and receive all the tools, answers, and especially the great gift they have within: a life of fulfillment, growth, and perpetual realization in every field of life that you choose.

The Key of Desire

Back to the Great Magician

"Deep in the soul of man there is an ancient temple, where lies the chest of hidden dreams, and guarding it is the great magician, waiting for the day when man will choose to return home with the key to all the answers."

The morning rose over the town of Pompeii as I was walking down the awakening street. A camera hung around my neck and all my senses were sharpened to catch the next moment. I breathed in the clear air and preserved the magic with my camera. The sounds of prayer enveloped me from every direction, echoing in the magnificent walls of the church. Its bells welcomed the inhabitants of the small town and placed them under the wings of faith. The voices of the praying crowd penetrated me and echoed an exciting discovery. Without understanding a word, I suddenly knew.

I felt another part of me had opened up. It awakened and revealed a great passion that had no name. I entered the church, as the priest's voice reverberated in the great spaces of a golden building, and I felt the great voice echo within me.
I am not a believer, but I have a great faith that has resonated for years in the chambers of my soul. I heard myself here in the holy sanctuary of a religion that was not mine, but it spoke to me in new frequencies.

Suddenly I heard an inner voice whispering to me, "Prayer is a spiritual way that allows a person to enter into his soul and discover endless worlds in it." It said, "Realization is the way to bring the prayer to light and to turn it into a way of life filled with passion and existential realization. Leave the known and familiar and go to the place where your soul awaits".

I stood among the crowd, closed my eyes, and gave myself over to my sensations, excited. "Somewhere along the way, people learned to live someone else's life, and you have lived like that for too many years. Now it is your turn. Get up and share your gifts with the world," the voice continued to echo in me.

I took a deep breath. Like a moving film, I saw images in my mind, the faces of all those who accompanied me on my path and were now gone. Those who left the world and those I chose to release so that I could fly as high as I can. There was heaviness in me and my sadness filled my eyes over what was and what I left behind. For one moment, I tried to catch those magical moments that had disappeared into the history book of my life.

"Welcome to the New World," the priest's voice sang inside me. "The eagle still keeps guard from afar, believing and knowing that you deserve your own flight. The universe worships the realizers, and now it is your turn to spread your wings and live."

I turned to the front door, "Thank you," I whispered in my heart and went out to have the breakfast that was awaiting me.

Awakening to desire

Along the journey that you have begun, you will need to find four keys that will help you plan your way and follow it throughout your entire life journey. To find these keys, you will need to perform different tasks, which will reveal the keys to you one by one.

The first task in your quest is **to find the key of desire**. **This is the first and most significant key, on which the Four-Key Method rests**. The Key of Desire is the key to unlocking the first lock in your hidden dreams chest, and it is what will enable these dreams to become reality.

Desire is the basis for everything you choose to do in your life. It is the only factor that really affects your quality of life and allows every person to realize dreams and live in perfection and self-realization continuously.

We spend most of our lives according to the paradigm that life offers us, as we have been accustomed to that life for as long as we remember.

We move within the exhausting and endless survival mode that society dictates to us and in the never-ending pursuit of money. Most of us choose our friends from social conventions. We take a trip after college or, in Israel, after we serve in the army, according to the current trends, or wherever our friends chose to travel to. We follow the dreams planted in us by our parents. Most of us choose our profession according to what will bring us the best way of earning a living and a wide range of extraneous considerations.

What about us? What about what really interests us and ignites our passion? What do we really want? What will make us feel complete and authentic? What if we dare to look inside, discover our inner world, and turn it into a way of life?

We can have a lot of money, be in a long term relationship, be the kind of people who seem to have everything, and still feel empty, lonely and deprived within.

As long as we do not wake up, put our own spark into our lives, and are not connected to our inner truth, we will not live fully.

The Key to Desire offers you an alternative way to access a special place where answers are available to all the questions that allow you to live in connection with that inner truth and connect with your true mission. If you adjust your inner listening ability and allow access to it at any given moment, you will gain a powerful tool that will be your compass and will allow you to keep to the road permanently.

Who are the big winners? First, it is you. And after you, in wide ripples, all the circles close to you and later the circles further away.

Thus, your destiny becomes your mission and the mission turns to great personal fulfillment. But more importantly, this is how the butterfly effect is created. The power of many people who live a life of fulfillment and passion is the ability to create real change on a global scale.

Now you are probably asking yourself how can you connect to this place and further more, how can you begin to live as your authentic self?

Let us start from the beginning.

As in most fantasy stories, our hero (who is you) lives a calm and ordinary life in a small village somewhere, unaware of his mission and powers. Thus, until strange things begin to happen around him and as he tries to understand, an unusual event takes place that forces him to embark on a journey and discover his true strengths, abilities, values, talents, and his real mission. So it is in fantastic tales. In our lives, it is a bit more complicated.

For as long as I can remember, I was a different kind of a child. I never understood what I was really doing here. Why did I come into a world with so much sadness and malice? Frankly, I have very few memories of my childhood. Mostly, I remember my feelings and the difficult loneliness in the children's home. I remember the caregivers who did not know what to do in the face of the constant harassment of my classmates and chose instead to send me to therapy and treatments with professionals. I remember a lot of crying and suppression of all my communication skills. I grew up to be a frightened and closed off child. I knew that if I spoke up, I would be humiliated. And so, I learned to protect myself by developing a mechanism of disappearance; Not to speak, not to dare, and not to stand out (which was not a simple task for a red-haired girl like me).

When I look back at those days, I see an introverted girl who thought she was not good at anything. To be successful meant to stand out and to stand out meant humiliation, ridicule, and physical violence. This lethal defense mechanism accompanied me until I went on to the compulsory military service.

I had only one girlfriend, and I clung to her with all my might, even after I grew up and realized that interests and extraneous considerations motivated this friendship. In the first grade, we both stood on the shore of the Sea of Galilee on a summer vacation. I remember how we each looked at the blue water and swore to be friends forever. So, the most significant thing in my life was that friend.

For many years, I lived adhering to that oath, blind to the cynical use and exploitation behind it. I was devoted to the friendship between us at all levels of my soul, but she was always there on condition. She was there when it served her and disappeared when I needed her. Again and again, she hurt me and again and again, I forgave her because of that old promise.

This is how my childhood and adolescent years passed, with a lack of belief in myself and total disconnection to my abilities and talents. Except for the talent of design and painting, I never felt like I was good at anything. I had never been chosen to lead, had never been deemed worthy enough to have a roommate in the kibbutz boarding school, and never felt I was of value.

The inability to see my true values blocked the purpose for which I came into this world and with it the gifts, skills, and abilities I was born with and through which I could fulfill my destiny here and live with fulfillment, satisfaction, and self-realization.

I had no idea what a great treasure I had within me. It did not occur to me that magic would break out of all this and illuminate other powers of the world one day.

Then enlistment day came. I packed my clothes into the bag and great excitement with it, as if I knew from within that something was about to be awakened. I did not forget to pack alongside the excitement, my own lack of self-belief and the elaborate mechanism of disappearance that I had mastered over the years. So we arrived at the collection station in Haifa. A group of weeping, grieving young girls, anxious parents, and I, with some unexplained inner energy inside me, smiling to the world as if seeing it for the first time.

With a hug and a kiss to my parents, I jumped on the bus, waving goodbye with a big smile on my lips and trying to understand what all the crying and sadness around me was about.
This is where my awakening journey began. A journey in which I experienced the challenges that forced me for the first time in my life to mobilize strengths and fight for myself, to use skills and abilities that I was not aware I had, and to begin to recognize my true value.

When people live their lives without being aware of their internal compass, they lose a part of themselves. At first it is invisible, and slowly as time passes, signs begin to appear. It can come in a variety of shapes; doors that begin to close in our lives and lack of success, unpleasant social challenges, a sense of inner discomfort, and more.

A large part of the world's population interprets the signs as the consequences of life and continues on its way, in total disconnection from the inner truth that is bubbling inside and looking for a way to break out.

But the more we ignore those signs, the more frequent and painful they become, to the point of actual physical illness.

Once we discover our unique basket of tools and connect to the same inner truth, we are born again and our passion awakens. This is when you have the right tools to enable it to come true, and suddenly there is nothing in the world that is impossible!

This is exactly what happened to me and **this is what will happen to you** as soon as you decide to commit to yourself and turn the use of your compass into a way of life.

As in that fairy tale, the moment our hero (who is you) discovered his abilities, a new awareness was born within him. He could never go back to being that simple boy. When a new awareness is born, a person we did not know existed awakens inside us, and a new journey begins.

Calibrate the internal compass

As you may have already realized, few of us are able to discover their mission in this way. Most of us go through a long journey until the day we discover our true calling or what I call, our life purpose.

But in truth it is not quite right because within each of you there is an ancient knowledge database that contains the answers to all the questions related to your essence and purpose. This knowledge shows you the correct way you are supposed to discover and begin your journey so that you can fulfill and realize your mission.

The amazing thing is that access to this database is always open to us. This means that if you adjust to the right way of life and remember to connect to that database regularly, you will be able to know exactly which way to turn at any given moment, what decision to make, and what to do to create successes in your life.

I call that database "the internal compass". While most people discover this wonderful reservoir only after an extreme crisis has occurred in their lives, I make sure to calibrate it every day anew and stay connected to it at all times.

The decisions I make in my life are made only after examining them in depth through my inner compass. The way to adjust the compass is through the Four-Key Model, into which I place every dilemma, difficulty, or decision that I need to deal with or make. This allows me to see the full picture, understand the way ahead of me, and examine whether it is right for me.

When you finish reading the book, you will also be able to calibrate your internal compass at any given moment and create an authentic and exact way of life.

One day, while I was sitting in the studio working on a new design project, the phone rang and on the line was Anna. Anna is one of the senior executives of a digital mailing company that I worked with at the time.

"Good morning dear," she said to me.
"Magical morning," I replied.
"Listen, I have got a crazy offer for you. Are you interested?"

"I am always willing to hear about new opportunities," I said and stopped working in order to completely focus on the details of the proposal.

"I have a potential new client from a big magazine. She is looking for a designer for the magazine, and I immediately suggested you to her. What do you think? Are you interested?"
"Of course," I said, and she gave me the phone number of the magazine owner.

Whenever someone chooses me, I get excited. I feel as if the girl I used to be wakes up and starts dancing inside me. I was chosen, I am good, I exist, and I am successful.

I already knew that when the girl inside me started to get excited, it was a warning signal. Somehow, almost always when this girl was excited, I found myself doing things on an impulse and without seeing the full picture. These were the moments when I was back to being that old Naama that acted out of the need to feel that she belongs. That was exactly the connection between my sad and exploited old world, and, the powerful, qualified, and connected to high-consciousness new world where I am a businesswoman, a mother, and a strong, happy and a complete woman.

I sat the little girl within down, asked her gently to hold off with the excitement, and picked up the phone. On the other end of the line, was a nice woman who said she was looking for a chief designer to work with. Someone who would help develop the digital niche for her as well as develop a new business niche in the field of business branding using the magazine content - Bingo!

"That is exactly what I do," I said. "I am a business coach who specializes in branding and business development." However, I explained that as I was a business owner, a full-time job would not be possible.

"Let us meet and see what we can do," she replied, and we set up a meeting. I got very excited. When we met, I found a well kept home and a pleasant, smiling woman. After we spoke, we reached an agreement of part-time work for the amount I dared to ask for.
We set a date for the work to start, and all I had to do was wait to sign the contract and become

the chief designer of a well-known magazine in Israel.

The girl inside me began to jump up with excitement, dazzled by all the prestige and glitz around the job description and the idea that I was going to be a major designer of a big, distinguished magazine.

That time I let her rejoice, but deep inside me a strange dialogue began between the happy girl who was given an opportunity and was chosen from all the other designers and the woman I am today.

The woman, who examined things in depth, did not rush to get excited before checking all the details, chose carefully, and only after examining the proposal from all directions, made a decision.

Something about the speed with which I was chosen for the job, and having to spend half a day in someone else's business made me feel uncomfortable. Something in my inner compass was indicating that it was not right. I could not explain to myself what it was, but it was clear to me that my decision was flawed.

Two days passed and the contract arrived. I always let the mature woman in me read contracts. At my first reading of the contract, I discovered that my fears were correct. The contract was one-sided, assured the rights of the magazine only, and included clauses that distorted what was agreed on between us. I asked the owner of the magazine to amend the contract, and the answer was a correction in the wording but not in actuality.

The internal struggle within me was difficult.

The girl in me was willing to go for it despite the bad feelings and lack of trust that formed even before we signed. She wanted to have a regular income and financial security. She wanted prestige, recognition of her abilities, and love from her surroundings.

Whereas the woman I am now began to understand that there was exploitation here, and signing the contract would dissolve everything I had built over the years. I would not really have time for my business if I spent five hours a day elsewhere designing a magazine. It might be convenient, but it would not be who I am.

Again, I sent in the contract, insisting on the clauses that denied me the freedom I needed and did not meet the agreements we made orally and waited for the correction.

Meanwhile, the first day of the transition into the job came and I arrived at the appointed time. She greeted me again with a smile and led me through the rear entrance to the editorial office. I was surprised to discover that all the glory and prestige I imagined dissolved into a dark, uninviting cubicle, and felt a knot begin to form in my stomach from the thought that I was going to spend most of the day in this place.

Suddenly, through the charming smile on her face, I noticed something else I could not translate into words and felt my body stiffen. The internal argument between the girl inside me and myself began again. One said yes to the opportunity and was so grateful for it, and the other said no! But I had already arrived and the work began.

The next morning I awoke with an intense pain. When the fibromyalgia wakes up, there is no room for internal arguments anymore.

When I let the girl in me win despite all the warning signs, my fibro has the last say. I could feel all the symptoms of the disease erupting at once. The blood changed the direction of the flow, the mental haziness was more pronounced, and every corner of my body hurt.

At that moment, I decided to sit down for a real dialogue with the girl in me and reach the place where I would make the right decision with which we would both be satisfied.

I connected to the Key of My Desire and examined the proposal. Did it promote and enable me to bring my values, skills, and desires into expression? The answer was divided. Yes, the value of creativity would be there but the value of freedom would be disregarded. What was more important? What fed what? What was the consideration that motivated me to accept the proposal? It was money. Was money a leading value in my life? No.

Would I be able to work in the magazine and preserve the independence, freedom, authenticity, and other values that were important to me in my life? Would I be able to preserve and continue the business I built with my two hands where all my tools, desires, talents, and dreams were expressed? The more I spoke with the child in me through the Key to Desire, the more we entered into the deeper meaning of the decision, and the picture became clearer.

If I went to work in this place, I would become a person with no light. I would sacrifice the entire enterprise of my life and would not be happy. It would be disastrous, and I would become a sick, nervous, nonexistent woman. I would become the girl I once was.

Along with the knowledge that I must not sign and start working at this place, a new fear was born.
What would they say about me if now, two days before the designer of the magazine left and I was to take his place, I retracted, bailed out, and

disappointed the businesswoman? How would it look in the world?

The outer shadows began to swirl around me and tried hard to move me back to the usual standard way. You committed! Now it is too late to withdraw! It will hurt your image, your seriousness, and your professionalism!

It was an inner conversation that combined body and soul. My good friend, the 'fibro', which became an inseparable part of my inner compass, stood on her hind legs and activated the alarm as loudly as she could.

I chose to listen to her. Knowing she would not let go until I did the right thing. So I found myself sending an email to the owner of the magazine, informing her that I was not going to accept the job, and would not be coming to the office that day. As expected, she was angry and berated me for my lack of seriousness, lack of professionalism, and unreliability, but I was determined to allow my inner truth to receive a place of honor.

A few hours passed. Slowly I felt how my bloodstream was circulating in the right direction. The pain was lighter and concentration and focus returned to me. A few days later, the phone rang. On the line was the magazine owner offering me a one-time design project for a client of hers, with a respectable pay of NIS 10,000.

This time I did not rush to give an answer and returned to the Key of Desire to check whether this was right for me. It was only after an in-depth examination that I approved and accepted the project and designed an amazing 100-page booklet to the customer's satisfaction.

This story is a classic example of what can happen when we do not listen to our inner voice and do not operate the internal compass from the beginning.

When choices in our lives come from extraneous considerations and do not serve our true mission, they cannot truly advance us.

And now the big questions arise: How can you know what your mission is? How can the Key of Desire and the inner compass help you find it?

We will reveal to you that the purpose of your life is an amorphous purpose that allows you to choose countless ways to achieve it. It is not related to the way you live, does not require you to engage in a particular field, and has no rules or frameworks. **Your mission is to bring a special gift to the world** and make it a better, more thoughtful, and more developed place.

The light that we create when we fulfill ourselves and realize our destiny enables the butterfly effect to exist and using it, we reach all corners of the earth. As more people wake up, understand what their mission is, become more truthful on their path, and work towards fulfillment, we will witness a fundamental change in the world.

This is the time to tell you about the Great Wizard. The part in you that guards the chest of dreams, waiting for you to reach it with the four keys, open the chest, and fulfill the dreams one by one.

This magician is also in charge of the place where all your tools, gifts, talents, and desires await you. You are already using some of them as a hobby or in doing business, but you do not always understand their role within your mission and may not be aware of some of them.

In this place, you will find the Key to Your Desire. From your special toolkit, you can also discover your formless mission and understand how to implement it in the most precise way, using all the tools given to you by the Great Wizard.

To be able to create fulfillment, be sure to stay connected to the ancient knowledge base, converse with the great magician, and use your inner compass at any given moment.

Make sure that you control the Four-Key Method and always return to the first key, the Key of Desire. As I mentioned earlier, it is the key that influences your ability to persevere in your journey of fulfillment and to bring your purpose into actuality.

The biggest gift shop in the world!

When a person is born, a private department in a large store is opened up for him with many shelves filled with gifts, desires, skills, tools, values, qualities, abilities, and powers. We often go into the big shop, look at the shelves loaded with goods, choose a gift for ourselves, and leave the store.

However, when we try to use what we bought, we are surprised to discover that it simply does not work. We do not really know how to operate it and do not really understand how it can serve us.

The frustration is enormous because we have acquired it with the clear knowledge that it is the best thing for us. Moreover, we stand amazed when we see that our neighbor has chosen exactly the same gift and that it works perfectly for him.

How is it possible? Let us organize it: This great gift shop contains the gifts of all the people in the world. Within it you will find many departments, each with a different combination of values, skills and tools. This way you will find identical gifts on different shelves. In fact, from the moment a baby is born, a special department is opened up for him in the large store, and the shop's staff makes sure to put in the tools he needs at any given moment throughout his life.

The period of adjustment in the army was not easy. It forced me to leave my comfort zone and begin to stand on my own in order to get assigned to a new base. My redheaded feisty nature, which I used until that point in time as a tool for unnecessary complications (in cases where I dared to raise my voice), began to surprisingly strengthen and create a new reality for me. So it happened that a few months after joining the army, I found myself managing a multilateral bureau and supervising a staff of four assistants.

I, the rejected, incompetent and untalented girl, was routinely entering the office of the chief of the Northern Home Front Command without knocking and saluting. Me!

Now I was in real trouble. Suddenly two identities were created within me. One was the soldier, the qualified manager, and the energetic responsible young woman. The one you can count on and had the ability to connect with people and be loved. And one was the person I turned into when my foot crossed the kibbutz gate. There were now two identities living side by side within one person.

I was confused. How can it be that the moment I leave the kibbutz gate I light up, magnetize people, live fully, and open doors to new opportunities. Yet when I return home at the end of the day, I dissolve into my disappearance mechanism? Once again, I experience the alienation to which I was so accustomed to in the environment that I live in.

The extreme difference between the two identities in me made me begin to explore the truth that was hidden within me and curiosity began to bubble in me. What was going on here?

It was in this period that I first became exposed to the existence of the great gift shop.
I was dizzy with the abundance that was revealed before my eyes. Every day I found a new gift. Like a child in a big toy store, I ran through the shelves and tried to play with whatever I could get a hold of.

Trial and error led me to know myself for the first time in my life. I became aware of the abilities, the talents, and the life within me. Often, during the long period of life that began during my time in the army and ended somewhere around the age of 40, I chose to use the tool intended for someone else. I kept failing and having great disappointments.

Every time I made a decision out of a place of societal pressure, the door to the big shop closed, and I returned to the starting point.

After my time in the army, many years have passed. I found myself following a boyfriend to South America, traveling by myself, building my life in the big city, working in various management positions, dating, having a family, and enabling my powerful identity to operate my life while the same old self that did not allow me to spread my wings and fly ran it.

During all these experiences, I kept walking around the big shop, picking up tools and trying to use them for my benefit. I was not aware that within this great, abundant store, there was one department that was all mine. In this department, I could understand my true essence and discover how to fulfill my mission.

I never imagined that I had a mission and purpose in this world. For many years, I did not know how to listen to my inner voice. I heard it, but I froze in the face of the possibility of getting up and rebelling against everything I knew. I did not dare to imagine my life being run by the same powerful identity that grew within me.

If you go into the tools, desires, and gifts shop without knowing where your personal department is, it is possible that the tools you have taken may not match your soul's code and therefore will not be able to serve you faithfully.

The role of your personal department is to provide you with the resources you need to live in fulfillment and to bring yourself into perfect expression.

Sounds simple? But it is not so. The various departments are not marked with a name or identity card and an unskilled person may approach the department only because it seems glittering or prestigious in his eyes and pick up the wrong tools. These will hinder him on the way and may wake up the shadows and the Hider of Dreams that lies within him.

What to do? In order for you to locate your department, collect the tools you need, and make it on your life journey, you must learn to identify it from among all the other departments.

That is exactly why you developed the compass that allows you to listen to your inner voice, which I like to call intuition, in the previous chapter. It is a loud voice that most people ignore until it screams and turns into a difficult event that aims to awaken them from a deep sleep.

Just like the fibromyalgia disease that erupted in my body after many years of trying to wake me up in a variety of ways and make me realize that I, like millions of people in the world, was just walking in the wrong direction.

This voice has the power to direct you to a new and fascinating world in which you can connect to your mission and from there to the department that holds your tools, passions, personal gifts, and the Key to Desire!

Just before you can determine that you have come to the right department, it is the time to do a little house check.

Take out your internal compass and make sure that the department is selected with inner precision and not from the shadows that are meant to stop you.

How can you ensure that you chose the correct one? Just before you choose to use a particular tool or make a decision regarding an opportunity (personal or business), ask yourself four simple questions:

- Did I choose the tool of my own free will or because of pressure exerted on me?

- Do I feel comfortable with the basket of tools in front of me or do I have doubt about the tools I chose?

- Does the choice empower me up or drain me?

- Does the choice move me toward my destiny and how?

If you have come to the right department, you can feel it charging you with power. Passion will begin to bubble within you and all you will want is to discover more and more tools and opportunities.

This moment, when you face your truth and look at all the gifts that are within you, is a powerful and exciting moment. At this moment,

you will realize for the first time in your life that you are unstoppable.

This is also the time to connect to your lifelines. Remember that you have the strength to accomplish the task and open the door to a magical inner world full of new powers and discoveries that will direct you to a new path, will allow you to create exactly the life you want, and fulfill your destiny and dream.

In the next chapter, you will discover how to create a new and groundbreaking consciousness using your tools, desires, and gifts.

Ready? It is going to be exciting!

The Key of Consciousness

When the big picture is revealed

"Wings do not belong to angels or fairies, they belong to the brave who chose to see the big picture and to walk in an endless journey of discovery".

This mountain! Only an hour ago I stood at the foot of this vast mountain, wondering what was the chance that, despite the 'fibro' and despite my shortness of breath and lack of physical fitness, I could succeed in climbing it? What strengths must I muster to reach the top?

I took a few steps and stopped to take a breath. The road ahead seemed endless. There was a heavy fog encircling me, and it seemed that beyond the wooden fence that kept the path secure, nothing existed. Only occasionally between the heavy clouds, could you see Naples across the Great Bay.

In the distance, I could see a wooden gate. I thought it marked the summit. Wrapped in the heavy fog, I tried to regulate my breath. There were just a few more steps. A wide smile spread across my face, and my heart burst with excitement. I had never felt so alive! Suddenly, I arrived! I conquered the summit!

I stood amazed at the view that appeared before me. Below me was a huge chasm in the earth, wrapped in enormous basalt rocks and an indescribable ancient power. In the distance through the thick fog, you could see the volcano vapor coming out of the active part of the pharynx, attesting to the life and power that was bubbling right underneath my feet.

The impossible combination of the remnants of lava that erupted here for millions of years and the green, growing, renewed vegetation left me stunned.

The fog was so thick you could not see farther than a meter, but just at that moment, I saw myself as clearly and sharply as I have ever been able to. Breathing deeply, I felt the ancient wisdom permeating through my body. I released my thoughts and allowed new knowledge to integrate into my consciousness.

Something began to thaw inside me. Right there, on the summit that froze an entire city 400 years ago, my powers began to reawaken. Thousands of insights descended upon me. Puzzle pieces fell into place, revealing my true mission, showing me the way, and signifying a new path for me.

"Sometimes, you have to let something inside die to allow the new to be born, and sometimes you just have to learn to listen to the heart key, the one who knows all the answers," whispered the big mountain.

"Look how much strength, how much courage, how many talents you received from the universe. Now all that is left is for you to jump in the air and start flying."

I looked at the mountain and could feel the lava inside of it rumble inside me. The mountain and I suddenly became one, and the excitement in me again disrupted my breathing.

"You have everything that is needed, that you intended to fulfill. You were meant to connect people to their truth. You were destined to be a light messenger in a world fighting for its existence." My eyes were bright, and I felt a new consciousness being born within me, strong, powerful, and all knowing.

"Just don't you forget," the mountain whispered to me. "The journey never ends. Many higher peaks are waiting for you to conquer. Never forget, you have wings and now you know how to fly."

Slowly my breathing returned to its regular rhythm. My thoughts were speeding. I made it. I succeeded! Now it was clear, I could conquer any summit. "I promise," I whispered back. "I promise."

As I began to descend the mountain, I could have sworn that I heard the mountain whisper my name again.

I breathed the clear air deep into my lungs, soaking up the magical beauty. One last photograph and I was on my way down the mountain to conquer countless more peaks, on the way to spread my light unto the world.

Turn insight into a new way of life

The Key of Consciousness is the second stage in the Four-Key Method. Its role is to transform the tools you work with into a new consciousness that will enable you to change the equation that runs you, plan the right path for you, and enable you to reach the goal you want to achieve.

It does not really matter what your current reality of life is and why you chose to embark on a new path of fulfillment. It is also of no importance if you are a business owner, an employee, or unemployed. What really matters is the fact that every change in our lives also requires a change in our thinking.

The simple and familiar equation is that 1 + 1 = 2 and it will never change. If you want to reach a different result, you must change the equation.

There are no shortcuts, no concessions, and as I have already said, there are no special magic potions in this process.

The only magic you have is the openness and courage to look deep into your inner compass to find the hidden connection between the tools in your toolkit, and understand what you have come to do in this life and what your real mission is.

On my 38th birthday, I sat at a cafe in Haifa, at a business meeting with a person newly interested in the branding processes. I met her at one of the networking meetings I have been dutifully going to since I started my business. At the end of that meeting, she came over to me, looked me in the eyes, and told me that she wanted me to do her branding.

It was a bit strange to me because then, at the beginning of my career, I was used to go through many assessments before I closed a deal. But she just chose me in the first minute.
That is how I found myself sitting with her in a small cafe and hearing for the first time about "super consciousness." As she was speaking, I felt that something deep inside me was waking up and it knew and contained the entire sacred scriptures. She told me about messengers that

came down to us to convey knowledge of creation and prepare us for the changes that are about to happen. She spoke of our true role in the world, the four foundations of creation and their role as a balancing force, enabling breakthroughs, and the precision of every person's mission in the world. I drank every word she said and none of it seemed odd to me.

As if I had just come from this world she was talking about, the more she spoke, the more I felt as if I have come home.

An hour's meeting had inadvertently turned into five fascinating hours that opened a door to a new, exciting and precise world.
The world she spoke of seemed to have been dormant deep inside of me for many years. That is how I celebrated my 38th birthday.

Throughout the branding process of that client's business and while writing a marketing booklet on the subject, I was privileged to be exposed to more information and open up to my internal knowledge base. Slowly, a new insight hit me. I began to understand what my mission was and for what purpose I had come into the world.

It stirred me with an intensity I could not stop. All my growth processes had accelerated in a way that inspired awe. Out of unexplained hunger, I started to ingest and learn about the world of super consciousness. I studied and learned about the foundations of creation, purpose and fulfillment, my personal path and the fact that every person has his own path, and we must not interfere nor try to change the life-journey of one another.

I was hypnotized by the new world I discovered and was even more captivated when I saw all this fascinating knowledge working in practicality.

I was changing rapidly before my partner's eyes and began to feel the gaps between us growing. The more connected I became to my inner world, the more I began to look with courage at the truth and realize that the relationship was wrong for both of us. It was not easy, but that was exactly what led me to understand that it was time to choose courage.

When things are right and authentic, they become a much less complicated story. Within two months, I found myself separated from my partner of the last 13 years. Despite the challenging decision behind every family breakup, I felt liberated and excited about what was to come. It was clear to me that I was starting a new chapter.

This moment in which you understand how the values that lead you in your life connect to your talents and unique qualities and turn into a burning passion, is the moment when something magical will begin to happen..

From that place, it is much easier to rise up and ascend to a new place. The moment that you understand the essence of your life and what it consists of, you can pack yourself a small metaphorical backpack filled with the supplies and continue on your journey to fulfillment.

Once you have created an initial connection between the Key of Desire and the Key of Consciousness, your next task is to learn how to turn the raw materials that you packed in your small backpack into a life-changing consciousness.

When you complete the task, you can receive the Key of Consciousness and begin planning the route you will take toward fulfillment.

The 'Altitude effect' - making groundbreaking decisions

Just before you approach the planning of a route and develop a strategy for your dream or business, it is important that you understand your essence in depth and turn it into a new consciousness.

When I say "new consciousness", I mean turning your spirit and your collection of tools into insights that can create a real way of life. Paving a way of thinking and developing a mechanism of precise observation of the world has the power to become an integral part of your daily life. These tools will accompany you throughout the journey from now to forever and will help you create any reality that you want without having to give up the authentic part within you.

To refine the idea a bit more, a new consciousness is the ability to transform your uniqueness as a person and business owner and turn it into a new way of life.

I was always afraid of snakes. As a child, I remember having a recurring nightmare almost every night. In the dream, a giant, gleaming, green-colored snake was chasing me throughout a classroom. I climbed on the table, and he came up behind me. I went outside, and he followed me until I woke up. He never caught me and to this day, I can still feel the great terror I felt then.

One day, in the early morning, I parked my bike in the shed near the dining room. I had a backpack on me. As I reached for the knapsack, a young viper jumped out and bit me. I was frightened. The bite led to the decision to cut my hand and attach a new hand to my arm instead of reattaching the one removed. I could feel the saw, how my hand was removed and replaced by another hand, and the fact that it did not even hurt.
I awoke and jumped out of bed in panic. What a nightmare, one that followed me all day. The alarm clock went off. It was 5:00am and another normal working day began. I got out of bed, got organized slowly, and headed for the laundry room.

On the way, I felt a sharp burning in my left wrist. The dream was staying in my mind, and I already knew that when a dream remained with me, it had a message.

I tried to remember the dream: a snake, a severed hand, and a new hand. What was going on? I got to work. It was very early and I was the only one there. As I sorted out the kibbutz's collective laundry and tried to decipher the strange dream, I felt the burn again in my left hand just where my hand had been severed in the dream. Reality was mixing with the dream, what a strange thing.
I looked at the searing place and noticed a small, faint red line across the arm exactly where the cut in the dream was.

I was in shock. Something real happened during the night, and I was not even sure I understood what it was. In fact, I understood but was afraid to explain this strange thing even to myself. Quickly I connected the dots.

That snake had been chasing me ever since I was a little girl. Once it used to frighten me with nightmares. Suddenly I remember a strange dream I had 15 years ago. Even then, there was a snake in the dream and something happened in reality after I awoke.

It was then that I understood I had a strange gift in which the dreams I dreamt would come true the next day. But that was 15 years ago. Since then, the phenomenon has disappeared, and I went on with the knowledge that I had special abilities that I did nothing with.
Something about that morning, in the dream and the stinging hand, was so different. It was clear

to me that something life changing happened that night.

Once you transform your essence into a way of life, you become a person who will always think of development and growth, strive to fulfill and accomplish, and will always walk in the right direction. That is where the mission, passion, and secret of true happiness reside.. It is in the exact place where you allow yourself to be who you are.

But how does this happen exactly? How do you take all the tools at your disposal and transform them into a new consciousness? And how can you discover your true mission so suddenly in the midst of life?

It is a bit like the chicken and egg question, and the truth is not absolute.

But in most situations, you can understand the mission from the totality and the composition of the tools available to you.

One of the techniques I have adapted for myself in life is to choose my point of view, and from a personal and multi-dimensional perspective, I like "to climb a high mountain" and watch reality from above. This allows me to see all sorts of ways and roads and discover countless new possibilities and perspectives. This is of course a metaphor, but it means expanding my range of viewpoints, thinking broadly about the range of options, and being able to see the full picture.

It is a bit like using a road map. If we get stuck in the middle of the jungle and try to find our way out of it, it is reasonable to assume that instead of getting out, we will venture more deeply into it. But if we have a map, all we need to do is stand over it, find North, and get out of the jungle safely.

In contrast to the roadmap, we have our special array of tools in life from which we can assemble the big picture.

Your basket of tools, composed as I have already noted from a range of qualities, skills, values, desires, and abilities, is the special essence that is comprised only by you. Here lies your differentiation as a person and business owner.

Since you have received this particular set so that you can realize and fulfill your destiny, it is also the key to being able to discover the big picture.

The big picture can be revealed to you in a wide variety of ways. It can come from a conversation with a stranger or a close friend, a book you have read, or a case that shocks you. It may be revealed by elements and situations that repeat themselves or from your ability to open up your toolkit, find out what it actually contains, and try to understand what the synergy is within each item in order to create the full picture for yourself.

For me, the big picture is usually revealed through dreams. Just like that night.

I began to understand very quickly that I had behaved with self-deprecation for most of my life. I did not think it was right for me to put myself in the center. According to super consciousness, I lived in the low energies. My whole life was lived from a narrow point of view. Usually this was not even from my narrow point of view, but from the narrow points of view of other people.

Only after I was very mature, was I exposed to super consciousness and began to grow and develop within my inner self. Only then did I acquire the ability to choose higher points of view that allowed me to see a wider understanding of life and discover my true mission. To be able to make the right conscious change and climb up, I needed a pair of wings.

The more I touched the sharp line that connected my arm to the palm of my "new" hand, I remembered the lesson about the foundations of creation. In the class, we discussed the snake as the symbol of the element of air. Its role within the elements of creation is to be responsible for the lofty insight and consciousness that enables man to understand the world from a broad and comprehensive perspective.

Now, like a puzzle, all the parts began to fall into place. A neglected, frightened child, closed off and self-contained within herself, flees from her great destiny. She cannot yet understand that the reality of her life can change if only she embraces the snake and lets it carry her.

Only after my military service and years after the snake stopped chasing me in my dreams, did I first go to live and work outside the kibbutz. It was then that the snake came back to visit me in my dreams.
 This time it was no longer chasing and frightening me but came to deliver news.

The air element, that for a long time brought me together with my inner deposits of knowledge and opened the door to a new consciousness, slowly penetrated me and allowed me to learn and prepare the soul for the great change at the right moment. And so that night I was given a new consciousness that had been assimilated in all areas of life.

Some of you might be skeptical about this story, but it did happen exactly as I wrote it. From that day on, something in my way of thinking changed. From a woman who used to observe the situation in a one-dimensional way and only through her own eyes, developed a more developed version of myself with a very broad system vision that allowed me to see far beyond the here and now and plan my long-term road.

This new feature brought impressive achievements in the management of the collective laundry that carried enormous debts. It enabled me to look at the range of possibilities that lay ahead and choose the right direction. Thus, a substantial change in my working method, procurement, and labor policy reduced the debts significantly within one year.

The new hand that gave me the ability to fly in my thinking significantly improved all areas of my life. My ability to always look at the overall big picture soon became my greatest strength.

More than once, when I dream a dream that stays with me even after waking, I make sure to process the information. I replay it and observe it from countless directions, in an attempt to understand what it is trying to tell me. I often wake up in the morning with the insight itself, sharp and clear.

On these mornings, I know exactly in which direction I should turn and what I should do next.

One of the most effective actions I take, when something along the path does not seem right for me, is to ask myself a question a moment before falling asleep. I usually wake up with the answer or at least part of it. This allows me to begin to understand what I have to do.

If I do not get an answer, I know that all I have to do is listen to my inner compass, where all the answers are, and continue to ask again the following night, gather the parts of awareness, and assemble from it the correct picture.

The mechanism of the keys is a complex function in which there is constant synchronization of systems between all of the four keys. That means that the Key of Desire feeds the rest of the keys throughout your life.

It allows you to have direct access to your shop and to choose whatever tool and gift you need, so you can nourish your consciousness with exactly the sustenance it needs.

The more that consciousness is attached to your desires and purpose, the more you can realize yourself and succeed in your life's mission.

To be able to find the key of your consciousness, it is important to be receptive to the signs on the way and to understand and absorb the messages and coordinates that will enable you to choose the right path.

A lesson in reading maps and signs

Being able to look at your world from an elevated perspective allows you to get organized and choose the right path for you. **But beware for there is also danger**: the risk of confusion and being tempted to walk on the paths not really intended for you.

From a once narrow perspective and that only had a path or two to choose from, you can now be able to see countless paths and directions and will need to find the right and precise path that will allow you to:

1. Realize your mission.

2. Do so with the tools, skills, and values you have.

3. Nourish your desire and create a life of fulfillment.

4. Be connected to your inner compass.

Just like the marked hiking trails around Israel and all over the world, on every path that you will go on, there will be signs along the way.

The role of the signs allows you to find the right direction and prevent you from getting lost.

Often when clients come to be coached, I find them confused, helpless, and not knowing which way to choose. At times, I watch them arrive at every meeting with decisions and directions that contradict everything we worked on in our previous meetings.

One of the main goals in the process of coaching and business development through the Four-Key Method is to restore my clients' confidence and ability to understand. Because only after they have understood what got them confused, can they go on any path they choose and plan it precisely.

My path too was and still is bewildering at times. Although I occasionally still choose the wrong path, I know that the signs will appear exactly at the right moment and will assure me if I chose correctly.

So how do you identify these signs? Let us return for a moment to those days when I started my own business, which in its first incarnation was a graphic design studio.

When I started my business, I had no coaching. The only thing that guided me was the deep knowledge that this was what I was supposed to do. I signed up for a networking group and started marketing by word of mouth (in those days the concept of digital marketing was in its infancy and I had no knowledge of it).

As I met with more people, I discovered to my surprise how challenging my task was and how I was lacking the professional and business focus that would enable me to clarify to people what it was that I was doing. In quite a few meetings with potential clients, after a long conversation and a detailed explanation of what I did in my business, the frustrating question would come up, "So what do you do exactly?"

I lived in between the feelings of empowerment each time I was hired and made money and the painful crash whenever my proposals were rejected.

I experienced this war of light and darkness for a long time. On the one hand, I chose to create a real change in my life. On the other hand, the shadows began to appear and tried to stop me from leaving that familiar place where I was small, hidden, and operating out of fear. It was like a warped dance. At times, the optimism led me and I became all-powerful, happy, and full of self-confidence with the knowledge that I can conquer the world. At other times, the shadows would take the lead, put the sudden brakes on, and leave me stranded in the middle of the highway rendering me immobile. Keeping me further away from the magical key that would unlock my personal treasure chest.

I found myself continuously on the dance floor spinning between hope and despair.

At that time, I was facing a troubling experience that almost brought me back to the starting point.

A client who was committed to purchasing a branding package from me decided, without letting me know in advance, to go with another graphic designer who was, at least in my mind, a colleague and a good friend. My ego started working overtime. I was greatly hurt by the client and felt my protective wall, part of which had already been removed, beginning to come up again.

I followed the two on Facebook for months, reading the posts and mutual appreciation they had for each other, as my stomach continuously tightened. The more that I contracted, the more I clung to Facebook. I kept reading and torturing myself and beating myself up without ceasing. I could not let go of the offense that settled over me, and it naturally affected everything I did on the personal and business level.

I started going on informational meetings with potential clients with a weakening belief, feeling like I was unprofessional, not qualified, not good enough, and countless other things I said to myself that cut through my soul. I was alone in this difficult place. My partner was not the person to share my professional difficulties with, nor did I have a business consultant to guide me on the way during that period.

The day of the announcement of that client's new logo arrived. She wrote in a great post that, which caused my stomach to tense as usual, that her new logo had been born after a long and professional process. As before, I found myself reading in depth the many reactions and congratulatory comments that began to be posted on the site.

It did not take more than three seconds for me to read the first congratulatory response before a comment was posted that the same logo, just in different colors, was already designed for a veteran company in Israel. Two comments below, another friend shared the fact that the same icon appeared in a free icon repository she came across on the Internet.

What happened next was so fast and powerful that to this day I can feel the power flowing through my body. Within seconds, I was pulled into my subconscious world and discovered where my true business power lies and what distinguished me from my colleagues.

Bright as the sun, I realized that I was developing businesses and creating authentic brands. The brands I created were based on the person's desires, talents and strengths. I created branding that fitted them like a glove and that no other person in the world would have, except for them. Later, I realized that I was branding businesses through their Key of Desire and allowing them to progress in an authentic business space that told their own story and created considerable business results.

That evening, I went to my networking group. As I stood up to present myself in the allotted 60 seconds, I chose to tell this story and present my insight simply as it was. "I am Naama, a graphic designer who creates authentic brands that are built on the essence of the business owner and cannot be duplicated."

It was at this meeting that the young woman who exposed me to superconsciousness, whom I wrote about in the previous chapters, approached me.

So what actually happened? For the longest time, I moved inside my business without a real path, without direction, and with no understanding of the signs that were put in my path. The obstacles I experienced, which came to me in the form of clients who did not understand why they should work with me, the client who left me and switched to another colleague, and the lack of success that was present in the beginning of my business, were not in vain. They all came to guide me on my way and to make me see my life from above, rather than the narrow and restrictive perspective I had at the time.

When I saw the signs, I experienced complete and utter bewilderment. In the absence of my unique basket of tools, of which I was not aware of at all, a barrier was created in me that grounded me in place instead of allowing me to move forward towards a breakthrough in my professional path.

Pay attention to what is happening in our life: the universe puts up small signs throughout our lives in order to open our eyes and awaken us to our mission.

If we are open to these signs, know how to read and understand them, and if we have the first two keys in the set, we can create and plan the correct path for ourselves and turn this plan into a clear and precise way of action.

However, if we do not possess both keys, we will have a hard time understanding the signs and interpreting them correctly. In this case, the signs will become clearer and more exact until we have no choice but to understand.

Now pay attention. The role of the universe is to wake you from the deep sleep, move, and motivate you to do the meaningful work for which you were born. The universe knows how to do its task faithfully.

It will never give up on you and will never let go. It will continue to show you what you are not willing to see until you are finally open to seeing it. That is why it is so important to be awake and alert and constantly seek out the small, delicate messages before they become extensive and real barriers to your life.

A mission can be expressed in a wide range of ways and areas of life. Which means that once it opens up to you and becomes your consciousness, you can create for yourself anything you want. As long as you are attentive to the external and internal signs on the way and make sure to transform them through the Key of Desire and the Key of Insight.

The secret ingredient to a successful consciousness

I often ask myself what the force was that brought me to such a substantial transformation in my life. What gave me the courage to break free from an unsuccessful marriage and start my own business?

What was this special element that enabled me to rediscover myself, in the army and on trips abroad to the unknown, and find out that I was a social creature and a wonderful friend, even though people in my life have always been a threatening factor?

What was there in those moments when I was about to give up, when I was about to fall, when I was afraid to make a decision, or when I chose courageously and discovered that my choice was a mistake? What was the secret element that made me get up again and again and continue on the way? In most cases when the question arises, I return to 1997 and my first trip overseas.

The self-image that had stayed with me since I was a child had not left me for a moment in the kibbutz society. Despite the great appreciation I received on the outside of the kibbutz environment, I was never given the opportunity to bring my talents and qualities into expression in my home and the place I was born.

Paradoxically, it was the volunteers on the kibbutz, who were the only landscape that changed frequently in the kibbutz, who actually saw me in a different light. And so it happened that most of my social life revolved around the volunteers, weather we were at their home, in the club or in my little room, but always with them. They gave me life and meaning in a place where I was not seen.

My dedication to every person who saw the good in me was complete, and from that place, true friendships were formed. These are the most beautiful memories I have from my life in the kibbutz. But with all the beauty and the life I received from them, every parting was a new death and each separation took a piece of me.

This was the case when Cecilia, a French volunteer who became my best friend and remains so to this day, left the kibbutz and I was left drowning in tears. It was the same one night at the airport when Martin, the great love of my life, disappeared up the steps to the plane and left me broken hearted.

I met Martin at a summer party in the kibbutz fields. He was the most handsome volunteer of all, and I was the one nobody loved. But it was with me, among all the young, beautiful, and confident girls, that he fell in love with. It was a true love story that crossed all boundaries of reason. We were together for six months until the day he decided to go home.

Three years passed. All the attempts to end our relationship and move on failed until a joint decision was made to reunite in Uruguay. I worked for a whole year in order to finance the flight. I was a young 24-year-old girl, utterly in love with a Uruguayan boy across the ocean, dreaming of a moving and sweeping reunion like an ending to a romantic movie.

And so with all these dreams, I got on a plane, making my way into his arms. It was the first time I was by myself, alone and about to face the great world outside.

The separation from my parents and family was emotional as none of us had any idea when we would see each other again. My parents cried and I laughed. I was happy. I knew that in 24 hours my love and I would be in each other's arms.

I did not expect for a single moment what would happen when we met again. As we stood facing each other, a little embarrassed, we were surprised to discover that our great love story had disappeared as if it never was. We suddenly found ourselves as if we were two absolute strangers. I remember the first thought that crossed my mind, "What the hell am I going to do now?" Countless thoughts ran through my mind at that moment, but nothing prepared me for the exciting journey I was about to have.

For two and a half months, I lived in his parents' house, sharing a room with him and a bed. Trying to believe that some of our great love would come back. But it did not happen. Martin was busy with his history studies and work at the family jewelry store chain, and I got a job at the main branch as a cashier and made a measly 50 peso a week.

The family accepted and embraced me. His parents were wonderful to me and treated me as a daughter, but on weekends I would be left alone, missing my parents, the nephew who was just born, and especially missing Martin, who was not there with me for even a moment.

One evening, unexpectedly, I made the decision to let go and return to Israel. Just before going back, I decided that since I was already here it was important that I use this opportunity to travel with the little money I had.

When you face a crossroad in life, when something does not work out exactly according to your plans, when you dream of more and cannot break through to the other side and change the result, this is exactly where the secret ingredient enters.

There is one factor that if you turn it into a way of life, there will be nothing you cannot achieve and that secret element is **the ability to be open**.

To be an open person means to apply all the tools we have gone through so far in this book. It means operating the internal compass, making good use of your toolbox, and always being connected to the Key of Desire.

Being an open person means to always look for what you do not know that you do not know, learning, and assimilating this new knowledge into your life.

To be an open person means to continuously create something from nothing. Find solutions to any challenge. Go on your journey with the clear knowledge that for a life full of passion and fulfillment, you must learn to recognize opportunities, be attentive to the signs and signals that the universe gives you, and gather the courage and determination to turn them from a collection of empty slogans into a reality in your life.

In order to make the decision to let go and return to Israel, I had to come to a place where I was able to look openly and courageously at reality and realize that the whole love story that lasted for the three long years was based on memory only. Living apart and in two completely different cultures had turned reality around and dissolved the strong connection that existed between us.

On the eve of the trip using the money I had left, I found myself facing a real challenge. I had never prepared for a trip to South America. I had no idea what to go see across the continent, was not proficient in the local language, and was about to embark on this adventure all by myself.

I booked a bus ticket to Buenos Aires and reserved the first night at the Back Packer in the city center. I packed a backpack with my belongings and started on my journey to the unknown. On the first day, I traveled with the huge backpack throughout the city using a map written in an unfamiliar language. It was challenging. I was alone but I was free maybe for the first time in my life.

I was surprised to discover nice people who were willing to help me lovingly, smiled at me, talked, and explained things to me. It was not in the repertoire of experiences I was accustomed to in my kibbutz. In the afternoon, I got to the room at the hostel, put down my bag, and got to know the other guests immediately. They told me a little about their plans and what there was to do. Through their stories, I began to learn about the place I had come to, and that was where my journey began.

For three months, I traveled throughout Argentina, Chile, and even a part of Bolivia. I travelled alone but was in wonderful company all the time. It was the first time I discovered I had social skills. I was surprised at how many friendships I had managed to acquire. There was not one person I met on the way that did not fall in love with the energetic, full of life redhead I was on this trip.

I travelled from place to place without a plan. I arrived, experienced, and chose when and where to move on. I got to know new people and socialize with them for a magical time everywhere I went. Because of this, I got to travel with a very funny English trio, with a group of fascinating Germans, and with many wonderful people from all over the world. I experienced a swamp in Bolivia, drank 'Mata' with locals, flew on a Paraglide, lived in an indigenous village in Chile, whale watched in Argentina, ate empanadas in the city of Salta, and broke through more and more of my boundaries.

At the end of the trip, I returned to Uruguay and reserved a plane ticket back to Israel. The night before the flight, Martin and I went on one a last date. While having a glass of beer in a local pub, I was amazed to discover the truth behind the story. He shared with me how hard it was for him to see that I was about to make a life in a third world country. He wanted to give me a future here but knew he had no chance of making me happy. He told me how much I had changed his life and how meaningful I was to him.

It was one of those moments where a person faces the truth and suddenly understands the whole story.

This trip was an enlightening lesson for me. I acquired great strengths and discovered that I am capable of being loved, cherished, and important to people. I realized I had leadership skills and that the world outside is much wider than I knew. The opportunities I have before me were greater than working in a dining room and lounging in the club every evening with a small and closed-off society.

I learned that all that is required of me is to be open to the world, to see the abundance of gifts I have to give, and to accept the many gifts that this world has to offer me.

Full of experiences that turned me into a new woman, I returned to Israel. I chose to start a new life in in the city of Tel Aviv, to discover more about the woman who was born within me, and to develop her as much as possible.

To turn the ability to be open into an integral part of your life, it must become part of your consciousness. Unlike other tools, openness is not a tool that sits in the bag and waits to be pulled out when necessary. Openness must be there every moment and every day, all of the time of your life.

Only then can you identify the things you did not know that you do not know and grow, whether in your own business or in your personal life.

Most people get up each morning with a routine. They are closed off and blind to the magical opportunities they have under their noses and miss out on life just because they were not receptive to the magic of the world.

And when I speak of magic, I am talking about two kinds:

Openness to our surroundings: This magic has the ability to simply spice up our lives and do our soul good, like seeing a rainbow in the winter sky, a small flower on a roadside, or hearing an encouraging word given to us in the middle of the day. This openness has the ability to simply make us feel good while on the bus on our way to work or while walking on a dreary street.

Openness to new opportunities and ideas: This magic has the ability to create real change. Openness can bring you to discover what your mission really is, what desires and tools you have received in order to realize it, and the way to make your new consciousness a reality at the same time.

How can you turn openness into a way of life?

1. Replace exclamation points with question marks and do not stop asking yourself questions.

2. Learn to recognize the signs along the way. They always come to help you focus and open your eyes to what you need to discover.

3. Be brave enough to know when something is not working and to ask for help.

4. When you experience setbacks, try to change the equation and do something new.

5. Create a wide range of perspectives that will allow you to see the opportunities you face. This will increase your ability to choose.

6. Do not let your ego control you. When something is stuck or not working, when you are confused or discouraged, get help from professionals who can help you reach the next stage.

If you use these six rules, I have no doubt that it will not be long before you become increasingly more open-minded.

Implementing all parts of this book up to this point will allow you to find the Key of Transformation that is waiting for you just around the corner.

Key of Transformation

Map of the Lost Treasure

"There, at the top of the highest mountain in the world, just as the sun rises, the greatest dreams are born, where each person begins his own personal journey of fulfillment, not with spoken magic, but with a collection of insights that have been internalized and become a way of life."

The alleyways of the quiet town nestled by the mountain on the island of Sicily were almost empty of people, despite the late morning hour. We went down the narrow streets, enveloped in their magical, old-fashioned atmosphere, taking photographs, laughing, and talking about my company Totem.

"You have to do something with all your skills," he said to me. I stopped in front of a large red door, trying to find the right position to catch it all in my lens and then turned to photograph him in the magic that enveloped both of us.

"All you need to do is hone what you have now, make it bigger, and add your photography to the game. You are an amazing photographer." I paused for a moment, listening to him and feeling something inside awaken.

It always moved me to hear that my photographs have touched someone else and that my ability to document the world from my unique perspective connects to people and opens up something within them.

It had been so long since I dreamed quietly of a way to share my insights with the world. I dreamed thousands of dreams but dared to fulfill only a small portion of them. Often, I dreamt about my photography but immediately rush to lock it up in my hidden box of dreams.

"I wish I had the courage," I said. "I am afraid that the desire to photograph will disappear the moment it becomes a source of income." He paused for a moment as we continued down the alley.

"Watching you as you photograph is a real experience," he said. "You cannot possibly lose this passion, it will never disappear, and when you photograph you are so alive." I smiled, yes, he was right. When my camera was in my hand, I felt the most alive.

"There are so many photographers far better than me," I told him. "But no one has the four keys," he answered.

"So what do you think I can do with it?" He shared with me the idea that came to him in that moment, and I could hear my heart begin to throb as a butterfly of freedom awoke within me.

Yes, it could happen. It fit with everything else and it is who I am! It would take some time. The idea would need to be honed, sharpened. and become more precise. However, it was definitely the direction to go in. "I can see it happening, complimenting my array of services, and giving me another way to realize myself and help thousands of people realize themselves," I said to him as we stop at the edge of town, just above the open sea. We looked at the great city on the mountainside behind us and the enchanting bay in front of us.

The butterfly inside me was fluttering and flying. The idea began to form, to become a real plan, not yet written down but clear and exciting. "Do you think it could work?" I asked him, letting the shadows envelop me for a brief moment.

"Who, better than you, knows that there is no such thing as impossible," he said.

How to become Architects of Dreams

If they told me eight years ago that I would have a business of my own and that I would become a woman fulfilling her dreams one by one, I would stop in my tracks and burst into laughter.

The gap between the woman that I once was and the woman I am today is so great that sometimes I look at reality and find it hard to believe that I am the lead actress in this story. At these moments, I try to find the point in which I have become an Architect of Dreams.

When I think about it in depth, there is not really one point where I can say, "It all started here."

So what brought about this big change? This change is the product of many small moments that create insights, which become consciousness that is then transformed into actions. Each small moment creates a new and flexible quality, which can be processed into one thousand and one shapes and colors.

My business life went through many incarnations and with it, my private life completely changed as well. You may say that I was blessed with a rare ability to reinvent myself over and over again.

Each time I discover something new within the Key of Desire, I am able to understand, integrate it, and turn it into a way of life. This is my greatest secret and that was how my business Totem was born.

In its first form, my business was a graphic design studio that dealt with all businesses that came to me. I had no business focus and could not explain to myself what I was actually doing. That is what happens when someone gets up one morning and starts a business without a plan and without roots.

Over the years, I grew roots while in motion, and it was not a simple process at all. I had to outline my business road map when the road ahead was dark. I experienced many frustrations in those early days.

Having a few successes after a large investment led me to understand that I must focus and find my precise direction. As this insight became sharper, I became more confused and less focused. That is how I managed the first year, and then the signs began to appear.

The first sign came when the seven-day mourning period, for the woman who had raised me for 30 years and was as a second mother to me, ended. I sat distraught in front of the computer and found myself typing two single words on the computer screen: "Inner Story". Without understanding what I was doing, I found myself shaping the words for several hours.

Only when I stopped to see what I was doing, did I realize the power of it. In front of me, I saw the next stage of my business. Just like Alice in Wonderland, I found myself facing a long road and seeing my new path clearly. I saw the uniqueness of my business, my professional plan, and the new basket of services and products that I had to build in order to fulfill my mission.

I felt the universe embracing me and showing me the way.

My first work association processes, within the "inner story" studio, dealt with graphic branding and the construction of authentic brands through exciting, focused meetings. My clients would come out of these meetings stunned by the intensity of the experience, and I felt myself becoming more focused and professional, especially within.

The signs did not stop and, between all the magic and satisfaction, I began to notice the cracks. I had very few clients and felt that this whole "inner story" idea was an up-in-the-air process that did not match what most business owners searched for.

I was looking for ways to turn the spirit into substance, so I came to learn about the world of digital marketing. Slowly I input the digital niche into my branding processes and created a marketing track for business owners, but that did not feel right either. I realized that it was not right for me to market other businesses. The right way was for me to help them create and do their own marketing.

Why? Because at the base of my agenda is authenticity and what produces all the processes of differentiation and business branding.

As the months passed, this sense of impreciseness increased. One morning, I woke up with the insight: I have to change the name of my business and from there the answers will come. I understood that my present name was right for a short period of time and came to connect me to the Key to Desire, to experience, to understand myself, and to turn things into a clear and focused professional agenda.

The time had come for me to find my exact way and create an array of services that will serve the new consciousness that had entered my personal and professional life.

I started looking for my business name, a name that will be professional on the one hand and will tell the unique story of my business on the other. I searched for months. I knew what I wanted to broadcast but could not find the correct name, so I chose to let it go and wait for the right moment.

Working with the Four-Key Method creates the correct synchronization between your understanding, your spirit, and the creation of reality of your life. It allows you to plan a "'realization plan" for any project you choose.

It allows you to pour your dreams into it and to actualize them. The Key to Transformation is the third in the Four-Key Method, and its goal is to turn your new consciousness into a road that is paved, planned, and as clear as possible. It is a way that will enable you to realize yourself at any given moment in all areas of life and become a Dream Architect.

In order to find the Key of Transformation, you must learn to translate the amazing tools that you have gathered for yourself throughout the journey and create a practical action plan.

In the business world, this stage is called the stage of setting goals and building a work plan. I like to call it the stage of creating the fulfillment plan.

In order to become Dream Architects, you must keep an open dialogue between the two keys you have already discovered. You have to make sure that each program, idea, and strategy is based precisely on your mission and desires and that you are making use of the personal toolkit that is available to you throughout your life.

Adhering to this constant dialogue, you will maintain an accurate synchronization and balance between your inner truth and the creation of innovation and maintaining a connection to our modern world.

To apply and live in real fulfillment, it is important that you practice the habit of returning to the Key of Desire daily and before any choice you make.

You will be amazed to discover that the universe is constantly giving you new discoveries and milestones because our universe has a fascinating quality. It can create a path of personal development for you and enable you to continue your journey of fulfillment continuously throughout your life.

If you have incorporated the Key of Desire, you have transformed it into a consciousness and a way of life, and you have built a realization plan for yourself. You have broken through to your next developmental stage. You are now ready to receive new information from the ancient knowledge database.

Once you are ready, know that the signs will appear and direct you on your way again until you understand and turn it into an integral part of your way of life.

Once I let go of the pressure to find a new name for my business, the signs began to arrive. It started with chance meetings and encounters I had with spiritual philosophers. I was constantly surprised to hear about my spiritual sources and what my mission was. It was always exactly the same. In a previous incarnation, I was an American Indian shaman. My soul was calling throughout my incarnations, telling me to help people live a life of passion and connect to themselves.
It was amazing! And that was exactly what I did in my business. So why had I still not broken through my glass ceiling? Why could I not progress and advance? I searched, excavated, and tried to understand but could not find an answer. Again, I let go.

Until one weekend, we went on a family trip. Being a professional photographer, my camera was always hanging on my neck on each trip. Upon our return home, I sat down to edit the photos from this lovely day.

When I photograph, I am completely into it. I only discover the real magic when I edit the pictures. When I see the photos on a bigger screen, the full picture emerges. That was exactly what happened that evening. My eyes caught a picture of a huge rock. Seemingly, there was nothing special about it. I just chose to photograph it because of the texture I saw on it.

But the moment I enlarged it on the screen, I was amazed to discover dozens of American Indian faces reflected from the rock. I was shocked!

I sat in front of the photograph and stared. Trying to count the faces without success. Every moment a new face appeared. An entire American Indian tribe came into view.

I went on Facebook and asked if others were seeing it as well or if it was only me. They were there, dozens of faces calling me to understand what was hidden from me all this time.

Suddenly I remembered that for a short period of time, I would take photographs of similar faces. Someone even asked me once where I found all those faces and how I managed to immortalize them in my photographs. The truth is that they showed up only after I took the photograph.

I understood it all the next morning. I realized I had to stay with my mission and the ancient Indian knowledge and create a method that will work on the spirit, the inner story, but would also know how to bring it down to reality and turn it into business results, realization, and fulfillment.

The questions that immediately emerged confused me. I asked myself how to accomplish it. I did not find an answer, so I chose to let go again and let it come to me on its own.

A few weeks passed. The new ideas circled around the question of what was the right name for my new business. Until one day, Totem came to me.

When that word suddenly appeared in my head, I remember stopping everything and getting on Google to search its real meaning. It was so precise that there was no doubt the big picture had been revealed to me.

What happened over the next few weeks was wild. My array of services and products crystallized and became clear all at once, and a new and exciting stream of clients began to arrive at the business. In six months, I had a breakthrough in my path and turned a business that was barely surviving into a successfully operating one. The revenue grew to numbers I did not even dare to dream of.

I have since been sketching out my plan of fulfillment again and again. Every time a doubt appears, I start looking for the signs, and once

I recognize them, I find myself in my next breakthrough.

Today, drawing up my plan of realization has become an inseparable part of me and my way of life. I sketch it in my head and put it in writing, which allows me to check off goals I have achieved and set up new ones.

If you are a new member of the Dream Realizer Club, I recommend that you draw up your own fulfillment plan on paper and allow yourself to assimilate it in a weekly or even daily process to make it an integral part of you.

An important tip for the road: While you are planning and building your fulfillment plan, whether it is for the achievement of a specific dream, such as a family trip abroad or for the realization of a broader dream, such as starting a business, finding a relationship, or developing a volunteer project, **do not forget to step up to an "elevated" place, and look upon the various possibilities available to you.** It is recommended that you write yourself motivating plans that will help you recalculate the route if needed while traveling.

Preparing an exciting program is especially important because, in its absence, you may find yourself stranded and forced to return to the starting point.

To start anew is an action that is required only in extreme situations where you discover that you have not synchronized the three keys assigned to the connection of a dream, a mission, or your plan for the path to fulfillment.

Put together a successful fulfillment menu

Just before you start building a fulfillment plan, it is important that you create a menu in which your essence and qualities are listed in great detail. This will allow you to see clearly the raw materials you are bringing with you on the path.

These raw materials will aid you in creating a detailed fulfillment plan. Before it becomes a whole plan that can be applied in practice, take a moment to put it all in order.

I recommend that you dedicate a special notebook in which to write your fulfillment program. Each time you choose to change and perfect it further, do so in the same notebook so you can see the transformation process you are going through while using the Four-Key Method. The results will amaze you.

What is on the menu? Your menu will contain a detailed list of all your values, skills, tools, and innate desires, along with the tools you have acquired as a result of learning and studying (cognitive tools and professional tools).

Why is it so important? Because it allows you to choose the resources you need to use in order to realize any goal, dream, or business activity you have chosen to achieve.

Just like in a restaurant, the menu allows you to order the best and most enjoyable meal. For you to be able to order a meal you'll enjoy, it is important that all options are available before you.

As you look at your personal menu, you can clearly see all the components of your personality and nature to the smallest parts. This position allows you to pave the way for success and to be in a continuous process of personal realization and fulfillment of your mission.

Your menu contains two parts: Inborn components and acquired elements. To maintain precision and constant connection to the Desire Key, you will need to return to it on a regular basis, at a time frame you decide on, and update it according to your own pace of development. Each time you return to it, you can
add more acquired tools and innate components that have been revealed to you.

As you continue on your journey of fulfillment, you can sharpen and bring more precision into parts of your fulfillment plan and leverage it to achieve new levels. You can add new ideas, personal dreams, action plans and self-realization, and new niches in your business. You can acquire a new profession and improve marital relationships, family life, and more.

The day after Totem's birth, I sat in my little dining room and began to concoct the renewed business. I quickly realized where I wanted to go, but I found myself alone facing the great task of building a whole business when all I had was a name and a moment of insight.

I was stuck again and felt the shadows begin to envelop me. They told me why I could not do it. Why I would not succeed and I should stay at the kibbutz Laundromat, where I was employed and had managed since I got divorced. It was an exhausting internal dialogue and was about to defeat me completely.

I was divided between the security of a small but steady salary and the desire that burned in me to give birth to the new version of the business and break free with all my might.

I had no one to consult with, and it was clear to me that I had to make a significant choice between the business and my work in the Laundromat. I could not manage both at the same time. I found myself wavering day after day without making a decision.

It was around the middle of 2014 when something in the unified laundry team I was running started to crack. I was summoned for a discussion in the human resources department of the kibbutz, where it became clear to me that all the support and affection I had experienced from the staff was only superficial. While I devoted all my energy to improving, saving resources, and streamlining the formation of the team, under the surface, the workers had a plan ready to remove me from my position by any means. I was shocked. I tried to bridge the gap that was growing day after day until I reached the point of no return.

Now I was at a crossroads. I needed to make a decision as to which direction to choose. When I looked back, I could see clearly all the signs the universe had planted on my path and how I walked by them all one by one, letting my fear for economic stability and survival blind me to it all. It was at that moment that I chose Totem, and on that day, I also chose to put myself in the center.

The first thing that was clear to me was that I was going to invest all my energies in developing the business and leveraging it to the place it deserved to be. After two years as an employee, the business shrunk in such a way that I chose to treat it as a new venture.

It was important for me to incorporate all the skills, loves, values, and tools I had into the business so that I would have a winning, authentic, and impossible to duplicate business recipe.

For that matter, I had to be precise in choosing the right business consultant. I knew that I needed an open-minded advisor who could help me bring my unique ideas into an exact basket of services and help me find the right marketing avenues for me. I looked for a coach that would believe in me enough to support my dreams, but who also knew how to direct me on my way and keep me from stumbling.

The consultant I found was perfect! We worked together for several months and created a collection of services and products that were affordable and accurate, and the most important part was that it allowed me to be myself in my business.

Each time the road you walk on is well planned and relies on the menu you created, you will feel energized and motivated to continue on the way to completion. This is the ideal situation in which a person moves from the stage of talking about, to the stage of taking actions. This is where you can enjoy the path even if it often brings you difficult challenges.

One belief that guides me in life is that the universe sends us challenges in order for us to become better and stronger and help us develop the muscles of courage, determination, and perseverance. Because only those with developed muscles can embark on the endless journey of fulfillment and flawlessly realize their destiny.

Once you have created a menu that includes all your unique ingredients, it is time to move on to the next level and create a winning recipe. With this recipe, you will build your own fulfillment plan and will finally be able to attach the Key of Transformation to your key ring on your way to the realization stage.

A moment before we develop your winning recipe. It is important that you adopt three basic rules that will allow you to create a high quality, perfect fulfillment plan that is connected to your mission and desires:

1. **The rule of Synchronization:** Throughout the process, make sure to synchronize the first three keys: Desire, Consciousness and Transformation. If you feel that you are stuck along your journey of fulfillment, have trouble moving forward, or have no energy, there is something off in the balance between the three keys and you have to go back to reexamine it.

2. **The rule of listening to the internal compass:** Throughout the journey, the internal compass is available to you and its function is to maintain a constant connection between all four keys. Listen to it and it will guide you on your way.

3. **The rule of openness:** We have already talked about this component. Be sure to include it in any decision making process and allow the signs to direct your path.

The recipe for fulfilling dreams

In our life, every program is a basis for change and as in life, it is the same in business or any field you choose to look at. So when you design your fulfillment plan, it is important to remember that the goals, the dreams, and the way to reach them and fulfill your destiny are constantly changing.

This is also why connecting to the internal compass and using your tools correctly is a central part of the planning process.

At this stage of the journey, you already know a lot about yourself and your pantry is full of ingredients that allow you to develop a winning recipe.

In your personal life, the successful recipe will be expressed in making right decisions, choosing a spouse, the way you educate your children, choosing the right profession, and in every other field of life.

In the business world, your successful recipe will be reflected in the building of a special way of working, developing a unique array of services and products, and having a unique approach to communicating and dealing with your customers, suppliers, and the people you work with.

To focus the idea, the successful recipe from which to build your plan of fulfillment must be based on your unique personal and professional program (the compass).
The program is the same approach that guides and leads you through life and expresses your special life force.

If you develop this recipe correctly and connect to the menu you have prepared, which includes your array of tools, insights, consciousness, and desires, your life will open up to new opportunities, growth, and development in directions that you may not have dared to imagine.

What is a successful recipe? If you take all the resources at your disposal and put together a correct mixture, you can create a winning recipe that will enable you to take a unique course of action and realize all of your dreams.

This is your plan of fulfillment and it consists of four factors that it are important to consider when you approach the process of developing a winning recipe:

- **Create a program guideline:** This will help you plan your course of action. The guiding principle is to know the specific "Why" for the project, the change, the service, or any dream and goal you have set for yourself.

- **Set the goal (the end result):** This is the goal you want to reach at the end of the road. The more specific it is and the more you are able to see it in your imagination, the easier it will be for you to create a realization plan for it.

- **Build a strategy:** Every recipe or fulfillment plan must have a clear strategy. The strategy is actually an expansion of your program and its role is to keep you from losing your way while on the journey.
The more in-depth and precise your strategic actions are, the easier it will be to deal with the changes that may happen along the way and recreate the route anew if necessary.

- **Plan the steps:** Set for yourself small, measurable goals for implementation. The smaller the steps, the more exact your way will be and you will be able to maintain high energy in real time. Be sure to connect the small steps with the big dream and with the variety of tools available to you.

Being a business owner, it is important that you carefully plan your business development phases. Define your collection of products and services thoroughly, make it a part of the winning recipe, and set for yourself small goals to implement the program, which will allow you to grow properly and over time.

It is very important to remember that each time you decide to create something new in life, you will have to go back, check the concept with the Key of Desire, focus with the Key of Consciousness, add new information that you have discovered in your menu, and develop a new recipe that will exactly fit the idea you want to implement in your life.

As long as you observe the four iron rules and be careful to include them within the construction of your fulfillment plan, you can carve out a precise and clear path but be flexible and able to recalculate the route if you encounter unexpected surprises on the road.

The more you carefully rely on the knowledge you have accumulated along the journey and make correct and creative use of the variety of special tools available to you from your department in the largest gift shop in the world, you will be able to fulfill yourself each time.

Throughout my business development period, I was enveloped in great passion and love when I woke up in the morning doing something that was miraculously me. Each action was coming from the depth of the Four-Key Method, which was born out of my challenging life story and from the need to deal with the fibromyalgia disease that threatened to completely disrupt my life.

The way of life I adapted to became, over the years, a professional tool that I have used in my work with my clients in the coaching, leading, and personal and business development processes. In one of my meetings with my business consultant, the idea arose to develop my own work method. It was funny that, despite the fact that I already had a successful work method and although I worked with it every day in my personal life, my business life, and with my clients, I was not even aware of it.

So it happened that I worked with the Four-Key Method for several years without knowing that I had exactly what I dreamed of. I have coached and led clients through powerful processes, turning them from confused and bewildered business owners into unique, focused business owners who knew how to use their own inner story to develop an authentic business brand.

I finally understood it at one of my coaching meetings with a client. He brought up his love for spirituality, and I was happy to share my spiritual way of life with him. It was the first time I had introduced anyone to this successful method that changed my life beyond recognition.

The client listened to me for a long time, and I noticed his eyes opening in astonishment. Everything was so precise and logical, despite being unknown and unpolished, for it was only at that moment that it became known. This moment that I suddenly realized that what I had been seeking for so long existed inside of me, was a powerful moment that is deeply etched in my consciousness.

Now, all I had left to do was turn the model into a work method and that is what I did. I was privileged to watch unfocused, bewildered people become real business owners. I got to see them become a brand, succeed in overcoming their fears and challenges, focus themselves, and most importantly, to sustain their passion at high intensities and renew themselves continuously.

That was when I realized that I was holding a successful recipe in my hand. This allowed me to have the clear knowledge that my purpose was to help people connect to their mission, to live in fulfillment, and to be truly happy.

Now, with a successful recipe for fulfillment in your hands, you have the Key of Transformation. You know exactly what you are going to do for yourself, for the people close to you, or for the world and how it brings you into expression and allows you to fulfill your mission.

The Key of Fulfillment

Fish Can Samba Too

"As substance in the hand of the creator, so is our soul, filled to the brim with the finest raw materials, and only the one who dares to open the hidden chest of dreams and listen to the melody of the heart, will be able to do the impossible, reverberate his gifts among the walls of the universe and have fulfillment".

A breeze greeted me as I opened the door of my room and walked toward the still, dark beach. The sound of the quiet waves played a love song for me.

With the camera in my hand, I went down to the sandy beach filled with broken shells and small rocks. I breathed in the fresh air, absorbing into me the wisdom of the universe. On the horizon of the wide sea, a new morning began to dawn.

Enchanted by the act of creation taking place day after day, I stood as tears began to flow from my eyes. Long months of pain and longing were removed from me in one moment on an enchanted Sicilian coast, and with it, understanding began to seep in.

The orange sun slowly approached the point of connection between earth and sky. Taking its time, confident in its eternity as only it can be. Between taking one photograph to the next, I saw in my mind's eye a series of moving images. I was walking on the timeline between dawn and sunset, painfully growing, having times of despondency and times of creation.

"Like the phoenix," a voice echoed in me.
"Dying in a show of flames and arising to life from the ashes and growing again."
"Where will I get my strength from?" I asked.
"From your very existence," the voice replied.

The sun began to rise up through the sea line, and I was captivated by the power and beauty.

"It is so big and scary," I said quietly as I look at the burning sky in the sunrise colors. "I am with you," whispered the inner voice. "A whole world awaits your gifts., Now is the time."

Far away in the sea like the act of creation, a new day was born, and with it, my mission reawakened. It was paving its way through the shadows, illuminating my way, ready to finally become a reality. A power I did not know was bubbling inside me. "Now is the time," I whispered to myself, and a smile of wholeness unfolded on my face painted with the colors of the dawn of my life.

Cast your bread; spread your mission in the world

This moment, which you are now facing, is one of the most exciting moments in the process of implementing the Four-Key Method. Behind you is the thrilling process of self-discovery, the development of a fulfillment plan that was born out of your mission, and the great moment of stepping into the application stage.

Now that you are right on the starting line, it is important that you understand what the word mission means. Your mission does not require you to do great work. In fact, all human beings are born with a mission of great significance and value to the world and to humanity, but each chooses the extent in which to perform it.

Therefore,, you can conclude that if you are truly connected to it, understand it deeply, and have turned your mission and work tools into a way of life, you are realizing it at every second, with every action you take, and every meeting and conversation with another person.

Your gifts, which have already changed from hidden into known and recognized, can now spread throughout the universe and create exactly the change you were meant to bring to the world.

It is true that when we talk about a mission, we immediately think of the famous mentors who have great careers and created global change and trends. It is true that mission is a word that is a bit heavy. This is exactly why it is so important that you understand, just before you set out and realize your mission, that doing something on a smaller scale is also wonderful, important, and meaningful.

As long as you are connected to the Key of Desire live in fulfillment, and keep your inner truth, the universe will continue to provide you with all the resources so that you can continue to spread the light in you.

Every step, every stirring of another's soul, every moment you live the mission itself allows the butterfly effect to exist.

Whether it is an honest sharing and the bringing of awareness on Facebook, helping a stranger on the street, or a smile and a kind word given to another for no particular reason and with no personal interest, every step can become part of your mission. **Realization occurs only when it touches another and creates change.**

On that 38th birthday in the little cafe, my mission awoke and began to seep within. It was exciting and thrilling to find that there was a reason for my very existence. This discovery led me to study and delve deeply into the super consciousness immediately after my divorce. I knew that the answers would come from it and the road would become more clear.

The studies created an intense development phase in me. Each class made it increasingly clear to me that I was part of that great consciousness and that I came here to disperse a significant part of its principles. The more this understanding permeated me, the greater the fear I sensed became. I felt the responsibility was too great. That I, this simple little girl, could not possibly do such a big job and give people the way back to themselves.

So when I had the opportunity to have a special channeling session with the super consciousness and learn the truth about the path of my life, the reasons that led me to my particular course of life, with all the pain, loneliness and fears, I felt something inside me close.

I was afraid to know. I was afraid to discover the extent of the mission, and even more so, I was afraid to discover that it was several sizes too large for me and to disappoint the great consciousness and myself.

But just as things always happened in my life, I found myself one day in a spacious house, sitting in front of the man through which the super consciousness teaching reached us, talking about our magical creation. It was an experience that was hard to explain in words.

There I received the answers and understood why I had come into the collective community of the kibbutz and a life of great suffering and what it had to do with my awakening now into my mission. I also got the confirmation that my mission should grow slowly.

It needed to touch people's hearts and make the right conscious change. I felt like a little fairy flying from flower to flower, opening the petals of human beings to the sunlight and showing them the magic within them so that they could begin to live their lives out of passion and connection to the inner truth, connect to their mission, and begin to journey on the best path for them.

I got home excited and started to think to myself, how? How do I do this thing? It was exciting and unnerving at the same time. There was a night of such great emotion that I had trouble seeing the road.
This experience made me realize that everything I needed to do the job was inside me and all that was required was for me to open my eyes and agree to see the signs.

I chose to release the fear and allow myself to experience the universe and its messages, with the knowledge that at the right moment, everything would work out in the perfect way, and I would discover the path I was supposed to walk on.

When you wake up to your mission, a kind of magic happens. The soul is filled with an unstoppable energy. It knows how to focus itself and tune the strings.

This awakening has its own rhythm. The breakthrough does not come all at once, so the smallest step towards it is a big and meaningful step.

This step is the first in a series that will increase and accelerate as you become more courageous in seeing the signs.

This is the time to remember the journey you have been through up to this moment, be wise enough to pull out the right tool at the right moment, and to keep your mind and your eyes open. Because once you are connected to it and your mission, the universe will begin to send you more and more signs, lessons, tests, and opportunities.

It will allow you to hone the mission further, help you dissect it, and show you the exact path you are supposed to walk on.

It is hard for me to put my finger on the day I understood my exact path. In fact, it was a road that was built so slowly that I did not even notice.

On the way, I have undergone innumerable challenges, experiences, and personal discoveries. Each time I was required to reconnect to the sources of my courage. I faced internal truths that frightened me, but once I accepted them and allowed them to exist within me, I experienced a perfect inner balance.

I found the places and people with whom I could let go, be vulnerable, and lose control, which enabled me to be more powerful and grow in the world. At the same time, I bumped into the shadows that threatened to swallow and render me immobile. Sometimes they succeeded, but by being joined to my truth with an unbreakable connection, which became a consciousness and way of life for me, I found the way to overcome the darkness, continue clinging to the light, and continue spreading my message to the world.

From that same precision and exciting process of connection and adjustment, I realized one day that I had a successful method in my hands. A method that had accompanied me throughout my life, grew with me, and focused itself over and over again. It brought me healing from my illness, enabled me to begin a new life time and again, to cope with a closed unaccepting community, to start my own business, and to find the point of light in all darkness.

The same insight had become a method of coaching and leading people. It brought me to work with fibromyalgia patients and help them improve their situation, lead business owners to build a unique, powerful and groundbreaking business, coach people to get out of their comfort zones, and move forward and towards a life of passion.

These days, the road that is changing and becoming increasingly more precise demands that I muster up the courage to break through my own boundaries, identify opportunities, and dare to grab them even when they seem impossible to do.

I know that this road will never end. I am standing in the middle of a huge playground where I can continue to grow and develop, dream more dreams, and fulfill everything I choose.

Over time, the insight became the exciting method presented to you in this book, "The Four- Key Method", which contains the greatest message of all:

There is not one person without a purpose, goals, skills or a mission; there are only

people who have not yet discovered the secret.

The Four-Key Method is a long-term method. In contrast to the thousands of instant approaches you will encounter in the market of personal and business development that offer mystical solutions, this method has no magic. There is work and constant connection between four layers that create for you the whole.

It is a method that requires courage and determination. Those who will wisely implement it will be constantly in motion and in the consciousness of growth, discovery, and transformation.

This method is a journey! The journey of a person, who will be brave enough to walk to its completion, get to fulfill his mission, live his desires, and be a person who influences his life, his surroundings, and all of creation. Once you have chosen it, the method allows you to cast your bread upon the water, with the knowledge that there is someone who is waiting just for you, and that you have the power to bring a gift of great value to countless people in the world.

Now that you have everything you need to achieve your goals, let us do the impossible. Let us go and find the Key to Fulfillment.

Look the shadows in the eyes

The journey of realization is now at its peak.

You are facing the path you have carefully discovered and planned. If up to now, you were required to stand courageously facing yourselves alone, you are about to come out and face the world and spread your truth publicly.

For 40 years, I circled around my path of fulfillment. When I was a child, I was light-years away from it, but as I grew older and discovered myself, I came closer to it until I found myself equipped with a rich and impressive basket of tools, filled with a great desire to set out and complete my own journey. I longed for the moment when I would find my own way, and I was sure that success would come with great fanfare.

From the moment I understood the mission of my life, I devoted myself entirely to that fulfillment. I made sure to teach my children authenticity, self-precision, and the development of personal abilities. I made sure to empower my clients, friends, and family as much as I could. I made sure, against all odds, to grow and develop while living in the same community that never accepted me and never supported my unique way.

Even while I was a mature woman and mother of three, who had an independent and growing business, I remained that small and simple girl in the eyes of a large part of that community. The wisdom of life and the mental maturity of the woman born out of the child I was, taught me to live emotionally detached from the community, to stop trying to fight for my place within it, to ignore the hostile gaze directed at me from time to time while walking around, and to build my own fortress of life.

I also received tremendous mental strength there, found my livelihood in an independent way, and cut off my financial dependence from the glass roofs of the kibbutz. Having great love for human beings, I developed a mechanism that allowed me to accept them as well. When members of the kibbutz community turned to me from time to time for professional help, I was able to look at them as if I had met them for the first time and discover their special appeal.

When I am asked why I choose to live in a place that has brought so much difficulty into my life, I take a deep breath and look at the question, knowing that there is only one answer.

It is precisely here, in this place, that I am asked to get up every morning, look in the mirror, reconnect to my truth, and remind myself that I am worthy, have great qualities, and am full of gifts.

Paradoxically, it is here in the darkest shadows of my life, that I gather faith, courage, and determination every day anew, allowing the phoenix inside me to rise up, spread its wings, and fly high beyond the limits of possibility.

To walk on the path confidently, take everything you have picked up along the way with you; your desires, skills, values, ideas, and your dreams.

Do not forget to put your inner compass around your neck and be equipped with openness and the ability to take off and look at the road from a bird's-eye view. All of this will help you progress on the path. The first steps may fill you with anxiety, but in order to go on, you will need to plan and pave the way while on the move.

Then take the first step! The first step is the most important. Once you have done it, something begins to move in the space of your time and place.

When you carry your fulfillment plan and your key ring, you can walk confidently. If you get to an intersection or get stuck on the way, all you have to do is go back to the Key of Transformation for a moment. Look at the program you have prepared and make sure that you adhere to it.

A note: When a person continues on the journey he plans, he will encounter quite a few unexpected surprises. As I have already mentioned, each plan is a basis for change. You will find often that your program, as wonderful as it is on the page, needs to be adjusted while being implemented. At times you will find that the reality is different from what you thought when you created your fulfillment plan.

In these situations, you will need to readjust the path to adapt to the reality you met on your way while maintaining your inner truth and desires.

The openness with which you set out on the path is exactly what will help you in these unexpected situations, and the universe will continue to guide you precisely throughout the journey.

So what to do when you get stuck on the road or encounter an unexpected surprise?

1. Return to the fulfillment plan. Remember that you have prepared an exciting program and this is the time to take it out and use it.

2. Find out what causes the difference between your plan and reality. Is this an internal factor that creates discrepancy within you, the inner Hider of Dreams, or are these the shadows that come through from the outside and try to

weaken you on the way, or are there circumstances beyond your control?

3. Once you have identified the causes of the obstructions, you can treat them properly. Handle and release the obstacles, then readjust your route, and continue with the new path you have planned or the road that opens up following the handling of the delaying factor.

4. All along the way, make sure that you are using the three rules I outlined in the chapter "Put together a successful fulfillment menu". Listen again and with an open mind to your inner compass. Create the required synchronization between your inner truth, desire and mission, and your consciousness of life. Focus yourself and only then choose your course of action and begin the journey stronger and with more precision.

The way of life that I have adopted for myself made me controversial, especially in the place I lived. Today I know that I have been this way from the day I was born. The close- knit community to which I was born became more receptive and open to accepting others over the years, but I remained the strange child few of them really knew. Most still see in an image that belonged to a very distant past. No matter how great the change I have gone through, however wide the gap between what I used to be and who I am today, here in my community, I have never been given the real opportunity to be me.

The shadows that accompanied me on the way and that were once a source of blocks, pain, and fear made me empowered today, stronger, and more precise. With a new consciousness, where every decision and every path I choose to walk on is connected to the powers within me and to my inner compass, the shadows turn into fascinating challenges and allow me to grow more empowered and stronger continuously. It is one of the most exciting processes a person can experience because it is infinite and brings me to new mountain peaks I never imagined I was destined to conquer.

You are now embarking on your way with you own special essence. You can apply in your life everything you have learned about yourself and everything you have dreamed of being.

You have everything you need to deal with any attempt to stop you on the way.

It is time to make a decision and stand courageously facing any challenge you will encounter throughout the journey. It is time to choose to live your real life, the life you choose for yourself.

As new people, you will meet the obstacles of your past along the way and your ways of coping will be different now.

Once you start living your life out of desire and fulfillment, the challenges become more complex, but the tools you have are powerful enough to enable you to stare deep into their eyes and be confident that you will not blink first.

This journey is infinite

One of the greatest dreams that accompanied me for 30 years was to write this book. While I sat and wrote for four months about myself and the magical work method I developed that had changed my life entirely, I often had internal and external shadows that rose up and challenged me to jump up another step on the ladder of growth and personal empowerment.

Questions like: What will happen if the book fails and does not become a bestseller? What if it succeeds and I find myself facing a wild successful outcome? What if I do not generate any interest? What will they say in the closed community where I live? Countless worries and fears that could have stopped me from realizing the dream surfaced.

These shadows are an inseparable part of every growth process I have gone through and will continue to go through my life. The great secret that keeps me on the road without breaking down lies in the kind of glasses I choose to put on and the optimistic points of view through which I taught myself to look at the world.

The deep familiarity with yourself that you now have and obtained through the use of the Four Keys will allow you to be confident in facing your fears and the public opinion that sometimes threatens to stop you.

Along the path of your fulfillment, you will meet all those shadows and the Hiders of Dreams, before you make the choice to join the Dream Realizer Club. But this time, you have the keys and if you will wisely use them along the way, you can create a powerful and empowering defense mechanism.

What obstacles might you encounter as you step into your path of fulfillment and how can you leverage them into growth?

- **Fear of failure:** Remember that in order to succeed on your way, many attempts must be made. Develop the approach that in order to experience one moment of success, you have to persevere, believe, and try again and again. Be creative and change your course of action whenever you get stuck until you succeed.

- **Fear of success:** Whether you take small steps or large steps, when you are well connected to your essence and the Key of Desire and are synchronized with your inner truth, you can always keep to your exact axis. Even when you become successful, you will be able to ensure that the same special essence within you will never change. It is the power of success to realize your mission and spread your light throughout the world.

- **Restrictive Beliefs:** Your limiting shadows and beliefs will come up every day. This is the time to make use of the tools and the new consciousness that you have adapted to yourself. Whenever one of your demons comes up and threatens to freeze you out, change the contents of the story. Create a way for connecting to your desires and the reason you set out on your journey of fulfillment. Paint an imaginary picture where you have already reached the peak, and remind yourself how powerful you are and what forces are creating that power. This will turn a limiting belief into an allowing and empowering belief.

- **Dealing with internal manipulations:** Daily use of your inner compass and the Key of Desire will keep you from the familiar technique of "telling myself stories". This consistency will allow you to remove obstacles that do not really exist from your path or to deal with the reality that you are trying to hide from yourself through internal falsification.

- **Keeping your determination and persistence over time:** When the map of fulfillment is in front of you and is based on your new consciousness, your desires, and mission, you will constantly create the eternal fire that will allow you to walk the path until you achieve your goal. Remember, the way is just as important as the arrival. This is where the wonders of growth and development happen and where you will become all capable.

- **You lack knowledge:** Study and learn. Sign up for a professional, cognitive course, or personal coaching process that can help you step up your development. Give yourself the ability to grow and develop all the time. Do not be alone in this. Our world is full of knowledge of all kinds and innumerable methods of work, allowing you to have the knowledge you need to create your life and live in unceasing fulfillment.

- **Social environment and the Hiders of Dreams:** The best method is to find the people around you who tend to stop you and instill fear in you and to choose, from a position of power, to release them from your life whenever possible. If these are people you cannot let go of, avoid sharing your plans and dreams with them. Remember that on the day you ascend the summit, they will be the first to stand up in awe of your success and applaud you.

- **Dealing with external manipulations:** The society in which we live, the people you meet along the journey, your family, immediate environment, clients, colleagues, or service providers, and people in general, are mostly driven by the mechanism that was similar to your way of life before embarking on the quest for fulfillment and search for the Four Keys. Therefore, in order to get cooperation from you or make you choose the path that is right for them, they will use a wide variety of manipulations.

Sometimes they might put their personal fears on you, as if trying to protect you, but are actually trying to ground you. At other times, they are envious or lack a basic understanding of the processes you are going through.

These manipulations are the greatest enemy of every person, and you are not immune to them either. This is the time to attach yourself firmly to the inner compass and make sure that every choice and decision you make is motivated by what is right for you.

Controls, as I have already written in the first chapters of this book, can come in a very wide variety of forms. Planting fears, creating guilt feelings, diverting you from your planned path in different ways, interfering with your relationships with other people, involving third parties in personal issues related to you, and more. It is important that you stay alert to when and where you feel uncomfortable and have trouble putting your finger on the cause. It is even more important that you carefully examine each such case on its merit using the Four-Key Method.

Be sure to ignore any manipulation once you have identified it, especially if it may divert you from your path.

It is important that you set clear boundaries in these places before the manipulations spill over into places that will hinder you on your way and bring you back to the starting point.

To do the impossible in life and business

The path of the Dream Realizer Club member never ends. After every dream you realize and every summit you conquer, the next dream will turn up for you. If you have reached this point, the Key of Fulfillment is already in your hands.

As you stand facing the horizon, it is time to hold the chest of hidden dreams and slowly unlock its four locks.

Now you can watch eagerly as your dreams are slowly set free, spread their wings, and begin to become a reality.

This journey is endless. At the top of every mountain you scale, the next discovery awaits you and allows you make further adjustments and choose another path.

There is no right time to start living and putting yourself in the center. There is nothing more exciting than the moment you observe yourself from the outside and realize how brave and wonderful you are.

As you watch this moving scene, it is important for me that you understand the meaning of this: From now on, there is nothing that stands in your way and you can be anything you want to be.

Going forward, you can achieve the impossible in your life time after time with the Four-Key consciousness, if you only choose to make it an integral part of you and your way of managing.

Using the Four Keys, you can improve any area of your life beginning with making simple decisions as to what professionals to choose so that they can meet your needs, to creating big and meaningful changes in your life.

If you wisely give the keys to your children, you will be able to nurture an empowered generation that can move mountains, grow, and have a life full of meaning and fulfillment.

The tools at your disposal are far beyond a spiritual cliché. They contain everything that a person needs to live a balanced and happy life.

This choice is the difference between living on the peripheries of life or experiencing it to the fullest. As millions of people in the world live their lives in a dreary routine and dream of other days, you have been given the opportunity to compose and conduct the melody of your life.

The next step

"You know, this journey changed my life," I told him as we sat on the shore of a virgin sea and built a pebble tower, waiting to see at what height it would collapse.

"I am going back knowing more, feeling more whole and more confident," he did not answer, just listened to me with a mischievous smile on his lips. "I have been looking for courage for so many years," I continued. "The right way to tell the world that I have a method that can overcome every obstacle and every challenge".

His silence allowed me to continue to summarize this impossible journey to which we had gone together, ten days earlier, three people who were strangers to one another.

"Suddenly I have words. Suddenly this consciousness that was hidden deep within me for so many years has become a method of work, a gift for countless people who, like me, can courageously change the course of their lives and be truly happy."

He looked at me and I knew that he was also excited. He could also see the magic that was born before his eyes. As the sun set slowly in the mountains beyond the sea, I could feel the phoenix inside me craning its neck and spreading its golden wings proudly.

This book is a great gift you can give yourself and the people who are dear to you. If you choose to embrace the complex ideas in it, find the answers that are deep within you, and dare, you will be given a powerful set of keys and strength. It will allow you to build your life out of an unending connection to the dreams you have given up on over the years.

I wish you great success in creating your personal fulfillment path and that of those closest to you.

In order to implement the ideas presented in this book, you will need patience, practice, and perseverance. As I always tell my clients and teach my children, **the processes of change of consciousness require time, training, and determination.**

If you want to study the method and make it into a real way of life, I invite you to learn from me personally on how to create significant breakthroughs in your life or business and turn them into a series of accomplishments, achievements, and a way of life filled with passion and fulfillment.

Contact me today and start creating the life you always wanted:

Phone: +972-52-5223421
E-mail: go.to.gdi@gmail.com
Totem's website: www.totem-d.co.il

The book "Fish Can Samba Too" is the first in a series of personal and business development and empowerment books. The series develops and expands on the Four-Key Method, and its purpose is to teach you how to use it to develop a successful business or fulfill yourself on a personal level. You are invited to follow the writing process and to purchase the books upon publication.

The Totem Company specializes in coaching and leading people towards the fulfillment of their business and personal dreams.

If you are a business owner or dream of starting your own business, you are invited to a Spot meeting. This is a unique consulting session that allows you to examine your business activities and discover how to build a groundbreaking brand using the Four-Key Method, as well as other supporting processes and models.

If you live with a sense of missed opportunity, emptiness, and dream of making a significant change in every area of your life, **you are invited to have a personal consultation** that will open the door to a world where change is not a dirty word.

The wheels of the plane began to move under the narrow seat, signaling that my exciting journey had come to an end. With my head against the window, Italy's enchanting landscapes began to slowly move away. As the views disappeared into the clouds, I heard a voice echoing in me: "It is time, girl. The world is waiting for you. Now is the time to conquer the next summit."

www.ingramcontent.com/pod-product-compliance
Lightning Source LLC
Chambersburg PA
CBHW071020240526
45469CB00006BD/2013